A

SPACIOUS

PLACE

POETIC DEVOTIONS THAT UPLIFT YOUR SOUL

DAVID KIM

Dedication

To my beautiful wife, Sharon, who has stood by my side for over three decades as my life and Kingdom partner. So thankful for your loving and kind presence. I cherish you!

CONTENTS

INTRODUCTION

> He brought me out into a spacious place; he rescued me because he delighted in me. (Psalm 18:19 NIV)

The Lord has brought us into a spacious place! King David penned these words in the Psalms as he experienced the Lord's deliverance in his life time and again. When he was at his wit's end, he cried out to the Lord. The Lord heard his cry and rescued him and brought him into a spacious place. The Lord does the same for us today! He has prepared a table for us in the presence of our enemies.

These devotional poems were written to be a spacious place for your soul—a place to find yourself and to meet the Lord on a daily basis. Based on the scriptures and personal encounters with the Lord, my prayer is that you may experience the goodness of the Lord through these life-giving words.

Chapter 1

Miracles of Jesus Poems

Jesus Christ is the same
yesterday, today, and forever.
(Hebrews 13:8 NLT)

I wrote these poems on the miracles of Jesus with this understanding: that the Jesus who worked miracles then does miracles today! I have personally experienced Jesus working miracles, including saving my life after I experienced an aortic dissection and rupture (less than 10 percent survival rate). He desires to do miracles in your life as well! As you read these poems, may the Lord increase your faith to experience a miracle from Jesus!

Water into Wine

> When the master of ceremonies tasted the water that was now wine, not knowing where it had come from (though, of course, the servants knew), he called the bridegroom over. "A host always serves the best wine first," he said. "Then, when everyone has had a lot to drink, he brings out the less expensive wine. But you have kept the best until now!" (John 2:9–10 NLT)

Jesus still turns water into wine! He takes ordinary things and transforms them into extraordinary things. At the wedding feast in Cana, Jesus transformed a crisis situation into a miracle that blessed many people. This is what He has done with our lives. He has taken our sinful lives and transformed them into His Masterpieces! He takes our ashes and turns them into beauty.

What in your life needs God's transforming touch? The current challenge or problem you are facing today is the very material that Jesus can use for a miracle. Bring it to the Lord today and ask Him to touch that area of your life. Praise God for His transforming power!

Water into wine
First miracle of our Lord
at the wedding of Cana
The apostle John did record

Wine ran out
at the wedding party
People having fun
Feasting was hearty

Mary called Jesus
asked Him to help
"If You don't intervene
We'll get bad reviews on Yelp!"

Filled the jars with water
and they became wine
Not just your average
but the very best kind

Jesus still does
Miracles today!
Miracles happen
when in His name we pray!

The Greatest Miracle

> The angel spoke to the women:
> "There is nothing to fear here. I
> know you're looking for Jesus,
> the One they nailed to the cross.
> He is not here. He was raised,
> just as he said. Come and look
> at the place where he was
> placed." (Matthew 28:5–6 MSG)

The greatest miracle is Jesus' resurrection! Jesus' resurrection confirms His identity as the Son of God. Because of Jesus' resurrection we know that the payment for our sins on the cross was good. This Risen Jesus is alive and well and encounters us today. Encounter Him in a fresh way!

Greatest miracle of all
is Jesus's resurrection!
Affected the whole world
Changed history's direction

After dying on the cross
Three days in the grave
Without a resurrection
We would not be saved!

Overcame the biggest
barrier of man
For everyone will die
has limited lifespan

When Jesus rose again
He gave us living hope
Now we have the means
with all things we can cope

The risen Lord is knocking
at your heart's door
To bring abundant life
To show you that there's more!

The Healing of Bartimaeus

> When Bartimaeus heard that Jesus of Nazareth was nearby, he began to shout, "Jesus, Son of David, have mercy on me!" (Mark 10:47 NLT)

We all have blind spots, the areas in our lives that need to be changed that we cannot see. Jesus brings healing to the blind spots in our lives.

Lord, help me to be aware of the areas of blindness in my life. So often I am blind to Your leading in my life. I try to navigate life on my own and I often find myself off Your pathway. So often I am blind to the people that are hurting around me. My eyes can be so fixed on myself that I am oblivious to the needs of people around me. Open my eyes of my heart to be able to see You, Lord. I want to be able to see You working all around me. As You enable me to see, I will obey Your leading in my life!

Blind Bartimaeus
Begging on the road
Heard Jesus was in town
Got in desperation mode

"Jesus, Son of David!
Have mercy upon me
I know You can heal
I know You can make me see"

They told him to be quiet
He shouted all the more
"I will not lose my chance
I know there's more in store"

Jesus heard his cry
Asked him the deep question
"What do want me to do for you?
What's your intention?"

"Lord, I want to see!"
Jesus granted his request
"Your faith has made you well
Go on your way, be blessed!"

The Woman with Bleeding

> For she kept saying to herself, "If I could touch even his clothes, I know I will be healed." As soon as her hand touched him, her bleeding immediately stopped! She knew it, for she could feel her body instantly being healed of her disease! (Mark 5:28–29 TPT)

Jesus heals today! The same Jesus who healed in the Gospels works His same miracles in the world today. He is the Same Yesterday Today and Forever (Hebrews 13:8).

The woman with the issue of blood had been suffering for twelve long years. She spent all her money on many doctors but was not able to find a solution to her miserable condition. She made a last ditch effort to get to Jesus for healing. When she touched the hem of His garment, she was healed!

Jesus, I come to You like the bleeding woman, desperate for Your healing touch. I ask You to bring Your healing in my life. Thank You for Your healing!

The woman who
suffered from bleeding
Looked to the Lord
to find her healing

Went to the doctors
and only got worse
Thought she was suffering
from some sort of curse

Broke through the crowds
Touched the Lord's hem
Was afraid of the people
Thought they would condemn

The Lord's power released
The woman was healed!
She bowed down in worship
Humbly she kneeled

Do you need His healing?
Call out in faith
Learn from this woman
who believed what God sayeth!

The Deliverance of Legion

> And as Jesus began to get into
> the boat to depart, the man who
> had been set free from demons
> asked him, "Could I go with you?"
> Jesus answered, "No," but said
> to him, "Go back to your home
> and to your family and tell them
> what the Lord has done for you.
> Tell them how he had mercy
> on you." (Mark 5:18–19 TPT)

The spiritual battle is real. The Bible tells us that we are all fighting in a spiritual battle against the devil and his forces. We need not be afraid, but we do need to be aware of the spiritual war. If we are ignorant of the enemy and his schemes, we can experience some defeat in the battle. The Good News is that the One living in us is greater than the one in the world. (1 John 4:4). Jesus defeated the adversary by His death on the cross. He gives to us His victory!

Lord, I will overcome it in Jesus' Mighty Name! In the spiritual battle, I will emerge victorious because of Your Victory!

Legion was
out of his mind
Tormented by demons
He was resigned

To a life of misery
Cutting himself
An isolated life
lived on the shelf

Jesus approached Legion
was gentle and kind
Rebuked the devil
Gave back his mind

"Tell your family
What I have done
You are a new creation
New life has begun"

A new disciple
was born that day
From Satan's prison
to follower of the Way!

Man by the Pool

> Jesus told him, "Stand up, pick
> up your mat, and walk!" Instantly,
> the man was healed! He rolled
> up his sleeping mat and began
> walking! (John 5:8–9 NLT)

Jesus, I desire to be made whole! The man at the pool had been lying in his crippled state for 38 long years! Understandably, he grew accustomed to his crippled state. When Jesus asked him if he wanted to be healed, he made excuses of why he could not be made whole. Jesus bypassed the man's excuses and healed him.

So often I get comfortable in my unhealthy state. No more! I desire to be healed! Jesus, bring Your physical and emotional healing in my life today!

Man by the pool
of Bethesda lay
Down by the water
Waiting for his day

When the water was stirred
He would be healed
His day never came
His disappointment unconcealed

Jesus asked the man
"Do you want to be well?"
The man made excuses
He was stuck in his shell

"Rise up and walk
You are healed today!"
The man rose and walked
God's glory was displayed

If you need healing
call on the Lord
By His stripes we are healed
It says in His Word!

Walking on Water

Jesus came to His disciples in their hour of great need-
they were about to drown in a raging storm. He came
to them walking on the water, bringing His comforting
Presence and transforming power. In a similar way, He
comes to us in our difficult times and brings changes to
our lives and circumstances.

Lord, I come to You today and ask for Your help to
overcome the present challenges I am facing with Your
supernatural power and strength. I can overcome all
things in Your Name!

In the middle of the night
In the midst of the storm
Jesus walked on water
and broke nature's norms

Thought He was a ghost
The disciples were afraid
They had not known
He was coming to their aid

"It is I," Jesus said
"So do not fear!
Time to kick your faith
into higher gear."

Peter left the boat
and walked on water too
Experienced a miracle
Got out of his pew

We too can walk on water
when we trust in Him
Let's get out of our boats
Let the miracles begin!

Lazarus

> Then Jesus shouted, "Lazarus, come out!" And the dead man came out, his hands and feet bound in graveclothes, his face wrapped in a headcloth. Jesus told them, "Unwrap him and let him go!" (John 11:43–44 NLT)

Jesus is the Resurrection and the Life! Lazarus was dead and in the grave for four long days! Jesus arrived on the scene and breathed His resurrection life into Lazarus and He came back to life!

Jesus brings resurrection into the dead things in our lives. Things that have been dead for a long time can be revived. He can strengthen the areas that are weak and awaken the things that have been dormant. Lord, I ask You to fill me with fresh Resurrection Power in my life!

Lazarus was sick
Jesus had delayed
Mary and Martha disappointed
How they had prayed!

Lazarus died
His body had decayed
He was in the tomb
for four long days!

Jesus called his name
"Lazarus, come forth!
In the eyes of God
You have great worth"

He came alive
Wearing graveclothes
For the time being
Defeated death, our greatest foe

Jesus is the Resurrection
and He is the Life
Putting an end to all
of mankind's strife!

The Second Touch

> Jesus put his hands over the man's eyes a second time and made him look up. The man opened his eyes wide and he could see everything perfectly. His eyesight was completely restored! (Mark 8:25 TPT)

In this miracle, Jesus' first touch was not enough. The blind man was only partially healed. He needed to bring a second touch to the blind man. This second touch brought full restoration of sight to the man. Oftentimes, we need a second and thrift touch from the Lord.

Lord, I need You to touch my life once again with Your healing power! I need You to touch my spiritual eyes again so that I may see clearly. Thank You for Your endless supply of mercy and grace that touches me again and again.

Jesus healed
The man who couldn't see
At the first touch
saw men that looked like trees

Jesus touched him again
then his sight became clear
The healer made
his blindness disappear

Healing methods of Jesus
Differed each time
There was no formula
for He is not confined

Sometimes we need
another touch from the Lord
That's what was needed
for this man to be restored

If you need a second touch
ask the Lord today
For He is the same
Forever and always!

He Still Heals Today

The same Jesus who did so many miracles when He walked this earth 2000 years ago is alive and well! He still does miracles today! He still heals the sick and still casts out demons. He is the miracle working God! His miracles are a sign of the reality of the Kingdom of God!

Lord, I put my faith in You and ask You to do a fresh miracle in my life. I need Your healing touch. Thank You for hearing and answering me!

Two thousand years ago
when Jesus walked on earth
He healed the sick
and offered a new birth

He made the lame to walk
He caused the blind to see
Does He heal today?
Is healing for me?

Jesus is the same
Yesterday, today, forever
His healing still remains
It's written in God's letter

By His stripes we're healed
God's Word proclaims
Lay hold of His promise
Jehovah Rapha is His name

Jesus heals today!
Lord, I believe!
I trust in Your love
Your healing I receive!

Mountain Mover

> Then Jesus said to the disciples, "Have faith in God. I tell you the truth, you can say to this mountain, 'May you be lifted up and thrown into the sea,' and it will happen. But you must really believe it will happen and have no doubt in your heart. I tell you, you can pray for anything, and if you believe that you've received it, it will be yours.'" (Mark 11:22–24 NLT)

Jesus is the Mountain mover! He told us to speak to the mountain and it would move. He has given us tremendous authority in His Name.

Lord, I speak to the mountains in my life and say "be moved in the Name of Jesus!" I say to worry, doubt and fear- "Be gone from my life!" Give thanks to the One who moves mountains on our behalf!

Jesus is
The mountain mover!
Watch Him perform
this God maneuver!

What's impossible
For us to do
is a cinch
in His view

He turned water
into wine
In the storms
He reclines!

What's the mountain
You're facing today
Causing your hair
To turn gray?

The mountain mover
Our God is here
Ask in faith
He won't delay!

Chapter 2

Wisdom from Proverbs

The book of Proverbs is filled to the brim with the wisdom of God, practical wisdom that gives us guidance for living our daily lives. Proverbs are meant not just to acquire knowledge but also to be lived and experienced.

These poems about the book of Proverbs have been written to help you experience the proverbs firsthand in your life!

Correction

> If you ignore criticism, you will
> end in poverty and disgrace; if
> you accept correction, you will
> be honored. (Proverbs 13:18 NLT)

How we need the Lord's correction in our lives! For me, receiving correction has always been very difficult. When I receive correction, it feels a lot like rejection. I get defensive and offended. I am slowly beginning to see that correction is a gift. Though sometimes not easy to swallow, it is oh so necessary for growth and transformation. May we courageously welcome correction in our lives so that we can become more like Christ!

Correction is hard
It hurts the pride
Yet it's oh so necessary
He won't let us slide

The Father disciplines
those that He loves
Addresses the things
we need to get rid of

To become like Christ
That is the goal
Sanctification
that we may be whole

Every tree that bears fruit
Surely He'll prune
To be more fruitful
No tree is immune

So, Lord, bring it on!
Correct me I pray
I'll humbly respond
and follow Your way!

Fear of the Lord

> The fear of the LORD is the beginning of wisdom, and knowledge of the Holy One is understanding. (Proverbs 9:10 NIV)

The fear of the Lord is the beginning of wisdom! How this is needed in the times we are living in. So many people just do and live as they please, oblivious to the consequences to themselves or to others.

To fear the Lord is to have reverence and awe for the Living God. It is not being afraid of God; it is to have a healthy respect for Him. When we fear the Lord, we do everything in our power to please the Lord with our actions.

The fear of the Lord
is the beginning of wisdom
Knowing the King
and life in His Kingdom

To revere the One
Who created it all
Our disregard
is the result of the Fall

To hate evil
and to love what is good
To do what is right
By His Word understood

Not cowering in fear
or running away
But loving the One
Who loves us always

Come fear the Lord
All the peoples!
We are His temple
The stars are His steeple.

The Proud

> Pride goes before destruction,
> a haughty spirit before a
> fall. (Proverbs 16:18 NIV)

Pride is the original sin. Man thinking that he knows better than His Creator. Putting himself in the place of God in his life. The consequences of pride are disastrous, leading to a disordered world.

Lord, keep pride away from us! We humble ourselves today before You. We acknowledge that without You we can do nothing. We draw upon Your strength and love to live our lives today. Thank You for Your mercy and grace that is poured out upon our lives.

The proud say, "I got this
I don't need to pray.
Like Frank Sinatra
I'll do it my way.

I can do all things
in my own strength!"
To push God away
They'll go to any length

To be in control
To be their own god
"I know better!
All others are flawed"

Pride comes before
You take a great fall
Only when you're humbled
are you able to call

on the Lord who can save you
Call on Him today
Seek Him while He may be found
He'll wash your sins away!

The Humble

God gives grace to the humble! The humble acknowledge their need for God in their lives. They recognize that we were created to live in dependence upon God and upon others.

The humble never stumble! Lord, we acknowledge that You are the Creator and we are the creature. We are humbled by Your great love for us. Fill our hearts with gratitude and may we never take credit for the amazing blessings that You have bestowed upon our lives.

The humble never stumble
Living close to the ground
They realize they're from the earth
In them, wisdom's found

The humble depend on God
Rely on His strength
Connected to the source
Living on His wavelength

Living with childlike faith
Not childishness
Taking God at His word
They live without stress

Humility is wisdom
A better way to live
Able to truly love
Willing to forgive

Choose humility
It's better than pride
Live with Your Creator
In Him, you'll find your stride.

The Rich

> The rich think their wealth protects
> them; they imagine themselves
> safe behind it. (Proverbs 18:11 MSG)

Riches are fleeting and are not a wise thing to bank our lives on. Trusting in riches is foolishness! Worldly riches are temporary; God's Kingdom is eternal. Yes, so many people gamble their lives away by putting their trust in material things.

Lord, help us to keep our eyes focused on the true riches of the Kingdom. May we be rich in good deeds and love. We put our trust in you, not in the riches of the world.

The rich trust in their riches
Foolish approach to life
Causes so much misery
Causes so much strife

The rich have false security
Think they've got it made
What will all their money do
when they are in their grave?

Worldly status is overrated
Lasts for just a moment
Much better and longer lasting
to be in heaven's enrollment

The rich oppress the poor
For this, they will be judged
For God cares for the oppressed
on this He will not budge

A message to the rich
Use money to do good
Store up treasure in heaven
Your eternal neighborhood!

Guard Your Heart

> Guard your heart above all else,
> for it determines the course of
> your life. (Proverbs 4:23 NLT)

The heart is the gateway to our lives. When our gateway is clean and clear, our life is blessed. When our gateway is blocked with unhealthy things, our lives come to a standstill.

Lord, help us to guard our hearts! Remove bitterness, jealousy, and callousness. Cleanse us by the power of Jesus' blood. As you cleanse our hearts, Your life once again flows freely in and through us. Thank you Lord for creating in us clean hearts!

Guard your heart
with all diligence
It requires
extreme vigilance

When the heart is sick
Life falls apart
For the issues of life
flow from the heart

Bitterness is poison
It is like cancer
Where to find healing?
The cross is the answer

Get rid of envy
It rots the bones
In God's heart
Abundance is known

Keep your heart soft
Keep your heart pure
With your heart in His hands
You won't go on a detour!

Wisdom

> The beginning of wisdom is this:
> Get wisdom. Though it cost all
> you have, get understanding.
> (Proverbs 4:7 NIV)

The wisdom of God is different from the wisdom of the world. The wisdom of God is based upon the eternal values of the Kingdom of God- His rule and reign. The wisdom of the world is based upon the premise that God does not exist. This is foolishness!

How we need God's wisdom today! So many choices and decisions to make. So many voices clamoring in our head telling us which way to go. Lord, we ask You for Your specific wisdom and guidance in our lives. When You reveal Your wisdom, we will gladly and quickly obey!

Wisdom is precious
More precious than gold
Will help you bear fruit
a hundredfold

Wisdom from God
Not the world's wisdom
The world is perishing
The prince of the air's kingdom

Insight for living
kingdom's wisdom is best
Will help you overcome
Any and every test

Seek out His wisdom
He freely gives
For He wants us to thrive
an abundant life to live

Value His wisdom
Don't take it for granted
In it, you're blessed
By His river planted!

Money

The love of money is the root of all kinds of evil. Money itself is not evil; it is the love of money that is evil. Jesus told us that we cannot serve two masters. We must make our choice to serve God and not money.

Keep us Lord, from the love of money. Money is a good servant but a terrible master. Thank You, Lord, for entrusting us with Your money to do the good works of the Kingdom. Give us grace to be good stewards of Your resources.

Money's grip is strong
Its traps who can avoid?
Money gives you options
Money fills a void

Money makes the world go round
So the people say
Can money bring fulfillment?
To money can I pray?

Money may buy many things
It cannot buy true joy
In the end leaves you empty
with so many toys

Money is a servant
It's a terrible master
Will leave you in bondage
Will bring you to disaster

Worship God, not money
To one master you must bow
To live freely with money
He will show you how.

Gossip

> A troublemaker plants seeds of strife; gossip separates the best of friends. (Proverbs 16:28 NLT)

Gossip is like a delicious, whole chocolate cake! When you eat it whole, you will get sick in your soul. It is so tasty and tempting, but it is not good for you!

Lord, keep us from gossip! Both sharing gossip and listening to gossip. It is so tempting to engage in. You give us a way of escape when tempted to share or listen to gossip. Show us the damage and devastation that results from gossip. This will help us think twice before engaging in it!

Gossip is so tasty!
Is junk food for the soul
Hard to take just one bite
Soon, you ate the whole

Gossip brings us power
People want to know
the secrets of others
They search high and low

Gossip leaves you dirty
Heart becomes unclean
It's like taking a shower
in the latrine

Stay away from gossip
Giving and receiving
When someone gossips
time to say, "I'm leaving!"

I am my brother's keeper
I won't kill with my words
I'll live with honor
Gossip's for the birds!

The Fool

> Fear of the LORD is the foundation
> of true knowledge, but
> fools despise wisdom and
> discipline. (Proverbs 1:7 NLT)

Fools don't know that they are fools, that is why they are fools. They act without thinking things through. They don't think about the consequences of their actions. And thus, they suffer.

Lord, help us not to be foolish in our ways! So often we follow the crowds and the ways of the world and succumb to foolish behavior. May Your wisdom lead us and guide us today. We acknowledge our deep need for You in our lives. Spare us from the pathway of foolishness.

The fool won't listen
to wisdom or advice
Thinks he knows the answers
He needs to think twice

The fool's unaware
that's why he's a fool
Doesn't learn the lessons
from real-life school

The fool talks too much
has too many words
Be careful!
Foolishness can be transferred!

The fool loves to gossip
About others he talks bad
Stay away from the fool
or to his number you will add

Listen! Be humble!
Don't be a fool
Read the Proverbs
and follow God's rules!

The Mocker

So don't bother correcting
mockers; they will only hate you.
But correct the wise, and they
will love you. (Proverbs 9:8 NLT)

It is so easy to become cynical in this harsh world that we live in. So much pain all around that affects us deeply. If we don't allow the Lord to heal our wounded hearts, we become the mocker that is described in Proverbs.

Lord, keep us from a cynical attitude! So many are jaded by religion and the church. Heal our hearts and make them soft once again. Help us to trust in You and in others once again. We truly need Your grace to do this. All things are possible in and through You!

The mocker is smug
Thinks he's above all
Tries to be bigger
by making others small

Heart has become calloused
Been hurt in the past
Filled with old bitterness
Die has been cast

Hiding in their pride
but wanting to play
Unable to break free
Alone he will stay

May I not be a mocker
Keep me humble, Lord
Keep me in conviction
when confronted by Your Word

There's hope for the mocker
God's love is the cure!
Hardened heart made soft
Once again made pure!

Trust in the Lord

> Trust in the LORD with all your heart;
> do not depend on your own
> understanding. Seek his will in all
> you do, and he will show you which
> path to take. (Proverbs 3:5–6 NLT)

Anything outside of the Lord will ultimately disappoint us. We put our trust in people, in things, in ourselves— all to no avail. May we wisely trust in the Lord and in His promises.

Lord, we put our trust in You! We lean not on our own understanding. We do not put our trust in ourselves or in our abilities. In our decision making, we seek Your counsel first and foremost. As You show us Your wisdom, we pledge to follow Your leading in our lives.

Trust in the Lord
with all of your heart
Seek out His wisdom
He freely imparts

To those who are humble
who know their need
Grace abounds
He intercedes

To those who are proud
and seek their own way
They'll get what they ask for
They'll keep God at bay

Lord, how I need you
Each and every hour
In my weakness
be my strength and power

I trust in You
Your ways are higher
Your will be done
It's my heart's desire!

Chapter 3

Poems on the Parables

Jesus's favorite method of teaching was the use of parables. Parables bring home the truth of God in a powerful way. They reach the head and the heart. Parables help us to see ourselves in the story and thus bring home the truth in a much more personal way.

Enter the parables through these poems! May you encounter God in a personal way through them!

The Ninety-Nine

Suppose one of you has a
hundred sheep and loses one
of them. Doesn't he leave the
ninety-nine in the open country
and go after the lost sheep until
he finds it? (Luke 15:4 NIV)

Jesus goes after the one lost sheep who strays. He loves the ninety nine too! Yes, He is concerned about the straying sheep, but He also thoroughly cares for the ninety nine who stay by His side! We are totally secure in His loving care. Also, the ninety have each other and have the security of the group!

In the security of the Lord and of the group, we can be at full peace. And we can have big hearts like the heart of the Good Shepherd. As the ninety nine, may we embrace our Lord's heart for the one sheep who strays and help our Lord welcome that sheep back into the fold!

To go after the one
You leave the ninety-nine
I'm part of that group
Will I be fine?

It helps when I remember
that I once was the "one"
My place is secure
I am a beloved son

Enlarge my heart, Lord
May it break for the ones
Who have lost their way
but are not yet done

There are so many "ones"
Who still need to come home
I will join the Lord's team
and bring back those who roam

A call to the ninety-nine!
Let's seek the one lost sheep
Bring him back to the fold
to the Good Shepherd's keep.

The Lost Sheep

At one point (or many points!) in our lives, we all were the one sheep who strayed from the flock and got lost. Whether we went far away or just roamed close by, we needed the Good Shepherd to come and rescue us.

Jesus always goes after the one lost sheep who strays! Even after we come back to the fold, we often stray again. The Good Shepherd goes after us every time we stray! We are so blessed to have such an amazing Good Shepherd taking care of us!

You left the ninety-nine
Came running after me
An all-out search
so I could be free

Though I was running
I couldn't outrun You
Your love chased me down
Finally broke through

When You first found me
I was a mess
Wounded and broken
filled with distress

You fed me and clothed me
Brought me to health
Now I am rich!
Enjoying Your wealth

Help me to find
other lost sheep like me
Who need to be cared for
Who need to be free!

The Lost Coin

> Or suppose a woman has ten silver coins and loses one. Won't she light a lamp and sweep the entire house and search carefully until she finds it? And when she finds it, she will call in her friends and neighbors and say, "Rejoice with me because I have found my lost coin." (Luke 15:8–9 NLT)

Jesus rejoices when He finds the lost coin- you and me! Because we were created in His image, God sees us as very valuable. He went on an all out search to find us when we were lost. So thankful for His perseverance in His search!

We are now called to join Jesus on His search for other lost coins. There are lost coins all around us waiting to be found. Let us experience the joy of bringing lost coins back to their rightful Owner!

Ten coins in the purse
One of them got lost
An all-out search
regardless of the cost

For the precious coin
searching high and wide
Won't rest till it's found
Searcher won't be denied

The coin has great value
though the Fall has brought decay
Created in His image
Imprinted *imago Dei*

The coin is you and me
We got lost at the Fall
The Father sent His Son
to find us, He gave His all

Be part of the search
Let's find other lost coins
Partnering with God
His cause let us join!

The Father of the Prodigal

> So he returned home to his father.
> And while he was still a long way
> off, his father saw him coming.
> Filled with love and compassion,
> he ran to his son, embraced him,
> and kissed him. (Luke 15:20 NLT)

The Father of the Prodigal is the hero of the parable! So often, the emphasis of the story is put on the prodigal son. But the real hero of the story is the Father, whose unfailing love shines through. He gives freedom to his son and lets him take the inheritance and leave. Then He patiently waits for His son's return. He runs to His son when He returns and welcomes Him with open arms. He throws a party for the lost son and clothes him in the finest clothes. He does the same for you and me!

The father of the prodigal
Waiting every day
For his son's return
Will it be today?

Brokenhearted father
Gave his son the choice
"Give me my inheritance!"
Said in demanding voice

He granted him his wish
His son went on his way
Living out his "freedom"
Life a big partay

Looking in the distance
He saw his son return!
Ran with all his might
With compassion and concern

Embraced his son with kisses
Threw a huge celebration
The father's heart rejoicing
filled with jubilation!

The Father's Love

So the young son set off for home. From a long distance away, his father saw him coming, dressed as a beggar, and great compassion swelled up in his heart for his son who was returning home. The father raced out to meet him, swept him up in his arms, hugged him dearly, and kissed him over and over with tender love. (Luke 15:20 TPT)

Rejoice in the Father's love! There's no better place to be in this world than in the Father's love. So often from our earthly fathers, the love that we received was conditional. We needed to perform and meet expectations in order to be loved. This has caused much pain and many wounds in our hearts. Our Heavenly Father's love is unconditional. His love is unfailing. His love is personal. It's for you. It's for me. This day, take time to soak in the Father's abundant love for you.

The Father's love
has greater reach
Covering over
every breach

Running to us
with open arms
His hugs and kisses
will disarm

Our defenses
and our shame
We are His own
We bear His name

Reckless love
Coming after me
His healing love
has set me free

In the Father's love
I am home
Where I am loved
and I am known.

The Prodigal Son

> "Let's prepare a great feast and celebrate. For my beloved son was once dead, but now he's alive! Once he was lost, but now he is found!" And everyone celebrated with overflowing joy. (Luke 15:23–24 TPT)

God loves prodigals! Each of us was once a prodigal welcomed into the loving arms of our Heavenly Father! There was a turning point in the story, the time when the prodigal "came to his senses. In that moment, he realized that it would be better for him at home in the Father's house.

In our Heavenly Father, we find our true home! With Him, we are safe and secure and welcomed. Going away from home makes us appreciate all the more how good we have it at home with our Heavenly Father!

The story of the prodigal
Very familiar tale
Living in the father's house
Thought he was in jail

"Life is better over there
I need to spread my wings"
Demanded his inheritance
Left with everything

Life was good, then suddenly
The money was no more
Found himself feeding pigs
on life's bottom floor

Moment of truth soon came
when he realized
Life is better at his home
This truth he did surmise

Returning from rebellion
His father ran to him
Welcomed him with open arms
New chapter to begin!

The Older Brother

> The older brother was angry and wouldn't go in. His father came out and begged him, but he replied, "All these years I've slaved for you and never once refused to do a single thing you told me to. And in all that time you never gave me even one young goat for a feast with my friends." (Luke 15:28–29 NLT)

It's so easy to become like the older brother in the parable. We can be faithfully serving God, doing all the right things and yet be living lives that are off track. The older brother missed out on the Goodness of His Father! So close, yet so far.

Our Heavenly Father welcomes us today to enjoy our relationship with Him! He is calling you to connect with Him at a heart to heart level, experiencing His love and deep acceptance. He loves you for who you are, not for what you do!

The less famous brother
in the prodigal son story
Is the sour older brother
in all his vainglory

Faithful in his service
Rich in good deeds
Small in heart stature
on his pride he feeds

Entitled and demanding
Unable to empathize
When the prodigal returned
him he did despise

So close and yet so far
Living in the father's house
Disconnected from love
He became a louse

Help me, Lord, not to be
The infamous older brother
I'll obey Your call
to love one another!

The Good Samaritan

> "Now which of these three would you say was a neighbor to the man who was despised by bandits?" Jesus asked. The man replied, "The one who showed him mercy." (Luke 10:36–37 NLT)

The Good Samaritan was just going about his business when he encountered the bleeding man by the roadside. He saw a person in need and helped him. How we need more Good Samaritans today!

There are hurting people in need all around us. We are living in times of division all over the world. We need Good Samaritans to love their enemies and show kindness to those who are hurting. Our world will be such a better place when we all stepped up to the call to be a Good Samaritan!

On his way to Jericho
a Samaritan passed by
Saw a bleeding man
The golden rule did apply

Bandaged all his wounds
Took him to an inn
Paid for all his care
Treated him like kin

The man helped a stranger
a sworn enemy
All this didn't matter
when he heard the man's plea

I am my brother's keeper
What if this were me?
I'd want someone to help
to care sacrificially

Let's learn from the Samaritan
How to love our neighbor
in deeds more than words
This is love's labor!

The Man by the Roadside

> Jesus replied with a story: "A Jewish man was traveling from Jerusalem down to Jericho, and he was attacked by bandits. They stripped him of his clothes, beat him up, and left him half dead beside the road." (Luke 10:30 NLT)

People are hurting all around us! Like the beaten man on the side of the road in the parable, there are so many that are deeply hurting and in need of care. The Good Samaritan was filled with the Lord's compassion, and this motivated him to help the man. The Lord is calling each one of us to be filled with the compassion of Jesus. When we are, we will be able to show the love of Christ to those who are suffering. This is the way of Jesus!

On his way to Jericho
when robbers beat him down
Bleeding and near death
Lying on the ground

Precious minutes passing by
Life was leaving him
No one came to help
Things were looking grim

Some religious people walking by
"Surely God's heard my cry!"
But they kept on walking
and left the man to die

Unexpected help
came from a known foe
A Samaritan rescued him
Compassion did bestow

Forever changed by the man
His precious life was spared
A lesson for us all
of a man who truly cared.

The Priest and the Levite

A priest happened to be going
down the same road, and when
he saw the man, he passed by
on the other side. So too, a Levite,
when he came to the place
and saw him, passed by on the
other side. (Luke 10:31–32 NIV)

Religion cares about keeping rules while neglecting the more important things. It's so easy to get caught up in our religious worlds and neglect the needs all around us. We can focus on our "spiritual lives", ignoring the fact that our spiritual life includes helping others in need.

May we learn from the example of the priest and the Levite of what not to do! Today, when you see someone in need, take the time to help that person. It may cause some inconvenience for you but this is what God is calling you to do!

The priest and the Levite
Villains of the story
On their way to "worship God"
their religion perfunctory

Saw the dying man
and walked right on by
"Surely others will help him"
Religion gone awry

"We'll become unclean
if we help this man.
That won't please our God
Must not be His plan"

Faulty reasoning
and selfishness abound
Caught up in their own world
heads buried in the ground

Look all around
and help those in need
Learn from the priest and Levite
Let's be a different breed!

Treasure in the Field

> The Kingdom of Heaven is like a treasure that a man discovered hidden in a field. In his excitement, he hid it again and sold everything he owned to get enough money to buy the field. (Matthew 13:44 NLT)

When we first met Christ, there was an overwhelming joy and excitement. Our empty lives were filled to overflowing with the goodness of God. The Good News is that we can rediscover the treasure of Jesus again and again as He reveals new and greater dimensions of His person to us! This is the beauty of the Christian life!

Today, may we discover the Treasure in the Field once again! Lord, reveal to us new aspects of Who You are in a personal and powerful way!

Treasure in the field
is the Kingdom of God
Found this amazing treasure
When I first found it, I was awed

Selling everything
to buy the field
Greatest investment
with the greatest yield

Purchased the field
so I could have the treasure
The worth of the Kingdom
No one can measure

The joy of discovery
Encountering the King
No way to describe
Better than anything!

Come buy the field
It's offered to you
Possess the greatest treasure
Blessings will ensue!

The Sheep and the Goats

> All the nations will be gathered
> in his presence, and he will
> separate the people as a shepherd
> separates the sheep from the
> goats. He will place the sheep at
> his right hand and the goats at
> his left. (Matthew 25:32–33 NLT)

The parable of the sheep and the goats is one of the most sobering in the Bible. Yes, we are saved by grace through faith. But if our faith is real, it will produce good works in our lives- like helping the poor and needy.

Be a sheep, not a goat! How? By caring for the poor and the hurting. What we do for them, we've done unto Jesus. There are opportunities all around us to care for people. Today, let's serve the people that Jesus has brought to our path. He will reward us for caring for the least of these!

The sheep and the goats
on Judgment Day
Will give an account
Their lives will be weighed

Caring for the poor
Feeding those who hunger
Binding up the wounds
of lives torn asunder

When we've done it to the least
we've done it unto Him
Shocking words of truth
that convict us of our sin

Opportunities abound
to serve those in need
May I love my neighbor
His command I'll heed

May I be sheep
May I not be a goat
I will help those in need
Spreading God's hope!

The Parable of the Virgins

> At that time the kingdom of
> heaven will be like ten virgins
> who took their lamps and went
> out to meet the bridegroom.
> (Matthew 25:1 NIV)

Are you ready for the Lord's return? The Parable of the Virgins is a cautionary tale for believers, challenging us to be ready for the Bridegroom's imminent return.

May we be like the five virgins who were prepared for the coming of the bridegroom! Jesus, our Bridegroom, is returning soon for His bride, the Church! May we be ready for His return. The best way to be ready is to enjoy daily fellowship with Him and to be fully engaged in His work!

The parable of the virgins
found in the Bible
Ten of them waiting
for the bridegroom's arrival

With oil in their lamps
Five of them were ready
They were wise
Their hearts were steady

Five were foolish
Totally unprepared
No oil on their lamps
Caught in the world's cares

When the bridegroom arrived
the wise ones rejoiced
Knowing they had made
the wise and lasting choice

When Jesus returns
How ready will you be?
Learn from the parable
and wait expectantly!

The Parable of the Talents

> The master was full of praise.
> "Well done, my good and faithful
> servant. You have been faithful
> in handling this small amount, so
> now I will give you many more
> responsibilities. Let's celebrate
> together!" (Matthew 25:21 NLT)

How we long to hear these words of praise from our Master- "Well done, my good and faithful servant. Let's celebrate together!" This will happen as we are faithful with what the Lord has entrusted us with. God has given each of us talents to be used for His Kingdom. As we put those talents to work for Him, God will reward us greatly! The Master is coming soon, may we be ready for His return!

Parable of the talents
The lessons to be learned
How to be ready
when Jesus returns

Differing talents
Given to each one
What is required
to hear "Well done"

Investing the talents
on behalf of the King
Used for His glory
Best return to bring

Don't bury your talent
Put it to use
Don't let busyness
be an excuse

Love your life fully
for the glory of God
This is the way
to make heaven applaud.

Parable of the Yeast

Another story. "God's kingdom is like yeast that a woman works into the dough for dozens of loaves of barley bread—and waits while the dough rises." (Matthew 13:33 MSG)

The Kingdom of God is like yeast...what a powerful picture of how God works in our lives! Sometimes we can't see God working, yet He IS working! Don't be discouraged when you can't see what God is doing in your life. Transformation starts small and then continues to grow. Little by little we are being changed into the likeness of Jesus day by day!

A little bit of yeast
Transforms the dough
into a loaf of bread
Causes it to grow

The Kingdom of God
is like a little yeast
Five loaves and two fish
turned into a feast

A little bit of love
goes a long way
Transforms the world
a little more each day

Yeast is small
at first you can't detect
It can't be seen
but you feel its effect

Be the little yeast
that penetrates your sphere
Bringing forth His Kingdom
for all to see and hear!

The Pearl of Great Price

> Again, the Kingdom of Heaven
> is like a merchant on the lookout
> for choice pearls. When he
> discovered a pearl of great value,
> he sold everything he owned and
> bought it! (Matthew 13:45–46 NLT)

Today, take time to treasure the Pearl of Great Price. Soak in the reality of this fact and enjoy His Presence.

Jesus, You are the Pearl of Great Price! You are more valuable than anything in this whole wide world. To have You is to have the Greatest Treasure a person can find. I am so glad that I found You! Rather, that You found me! In You, I am satisfied and filled with joy!

Lord, You are
the Pearl of Great Price
of highest value
Worth every sacrifice

Worthy of worship
Your beauty astounds
in Your presence
Your mercy abounds

For the merchant
with pearls on his mind
The Pearl of Great Price
is a matchless find

All else can never
ever compare
Jesus is better
far more rare

Than all of the treasures
Found on the earth
Jesus is singular
Incomparable His worth

Pearl of Great Price
So glad to have found
Jesus is Lord
Crowned with many crowns.

Chapter 4

Personified

The Bible covers the whole range of human experience and emotions. These personified poems take qualities and characteristics found in the scriptures and personalizes them using the first-person point of view. In so doing, the hope is that you will personally experience and embrace these many different emotions and qualities.

I Am Perseverance

> Therefore, since we are surrounded by such a great cloud of witnesses, let us throw off everything that hinders and the sin that so easily entangles. And let us run with perseverance the race marked out for us. (Hebrews 12:1 NIV)

Perseverance never quits! Jesus persevered through opposition and difficulty and completed His mission by dying on the Cross. Followers of Jesus can find this same perseverance through the power of the Holy Spirit.

I won't quit, Lord! In the tough times, strengthen me Lord and hold on to me. You won't let go. Because of Your great love, I am able to persevere!

I am Perseverance
I will not quit
I will not back down
once I commit

My motto is
Keep on keeping on!
For I am running
Life's marathon!

When the going gets tough
I get going!
In the grind
my juices are flowing!

I run on God's strength
He keeps me steady
His power keeps me
Always ready

I am Perseverance
Day by day
Pressing forward
I'm here to stay!

I Am Kindness

> Or do you show contempt
> for the riches of his kindness,
> forbearance and patience, not
> realizing that God's kindness
> is intended to lead you to
> repentance? (Romans 2:4 NIV)

This world needs more of God's Kindness! We live in an unkind world that is divided and at enmity with one another. When people opposed Jesus and threw insults at Him, He was kind in return. When Jesus was on the cross, He asked the Father to forgive the people who crucified Him. It is the Kindness of the Lord that brings people to repentance. May I be a conduit of the Lord's kindness to people around me today.

I am Kindness
Look to me
in the midst of this world's
cruelty

Divided times
we're living in
Due to "news"
and all its spin

Kindness breaks
the winter chill
between enemies
Spreads goodwill

Don't you like
to be shown kindness?
Do the same
and heal hate's blindness

I am Kindness
I shine my rays
Feel the warmth
from my gaze.

I Am Patience

> Patient endurance is what you need now, so that you will continue to do God's will. Then you will receive all that he has promised. (Hebrews 10:36 NLT)

Patience is a powerful and rare virtue. Thank God for His amazing patience towards us, forgiving us each time we sin and fall short. He is a loving Father who is patient with His children.

Thank You Lord for your unending patience toward me. You accept me with all my flaws and faults. With the patience You have for me, I choose to be patient with others.

I am Patience
So needed now
in troubled times
I'll show you how

To not give up
when you fail
When you fall down
I will not bail

I'm waiting for prodigals
to come home
Suffering silently
while they roam

Life's not a sprint
It's a marathon
So draw from me
to keep going on!

I am Patience
I'm here for you
So please be patient
with others too!

I Am Peace

> Peace I leave with you; my peace
> I give you. I do not give to you
> as the world gives. Do not let
> your hearts be troubled and do
> not be afraid. (John 14:27 NIV)

How this world needs Your peace, Lord! Most importantly, this world needs peace with God. This was made possible through the blood that Jesus shed on the cross. Secondly, the world needs peace with one another. This happens as people are reconciled to God and are then given the resources for peace. Finally, we need peace within ourselves. When we are at peace with God, His peace fills our hearts so we can be at peace within. As we receive this gift of your peace, we heed the call to be peacemakers in our troubled world.

I am Peace
Live in me
Come to know
Experientially

I'll guard your heart
and your mind
I'm not the same
as the worldly kind

I am a gift
Given from above
I come from God
the One who loves

Understanding
I surpass
When your flag is flying
at half-mast

I am Peace
Call on me
Take my hand
Live carefree.

I Am Love

Love never gives up, never loses
faith, is always hopeful, and endures
through every circumstance.
(1 Corinthians 13:7 NLT)

Human love will disappoint and fail us. God's love never fails!
This is what we need more than anything else in this
world. This is what we were made for- Love! To be loved
by God and then to let His love flow from us to others.

Lord, pour out Your love upon us afresh so that we may
live the life that is truly worth living!

I am Love
I never fail
Try to stop me
to no avail

I am patient
I am kind
I come from God
I am divine

I forgive
Seventy times seven
on earth
as it is in heaven

In me you find
Your soul's rest
I bring comfort
to the oppressed

I am Love
I outpour
I'm the Lion of Judah
Hear me roar!

I Am Hope

> And this hope will not lead to disappointment. For we know how dearly God loves us, because he has given us the Holy Spirit to fill our hearts with his love. (Romans 5:5 NLT)

God's hope never disappoints us! Worldly hope is wishful thinking. It may or may not come to pass. We are often disappointed by the hope we have placed in the world.

God's hope is based on the unshakeable promises found in God's Word. God is always faithful to keep His promises towards His children. It is hope that we can bank our lives on. This hope is an anchor for our souls!

I am Hope
Feel my power
So very needed
in this hour

In the darkness
When things look grim
I'll fill you up
to the brim

With buoyancy and strength
You can endure
Not wishful thinking
I am sure

I am the anchor
for your soul
With me, there is
no need for polls

I am Hope
I never fail
Live with confidence
on my rails.

I Am Faith

> And it is impossible to please God without faith. Anyone who wants to come to him must believe that God exists and that he rewards those who sincerely seek him. (Hebrews 11:6 NLT)

We are called to walk by faith and not by sight. Faith is spiritual sight that enables us to grasp the things of the Kingdom.

Increase my faith, Lord! Help me to take You at Your Word and believe the amazing promises that You have for my life. I put my trust in You. I will live by my faith in You and follow You when I cannot see with my natural vision.

You see a problem
I see possibility
I am Faith
Come see what I see

I see another realm
The Kingdom of God
The secular view
is surely flawed

I see God working
All things for good
This is reality
Not a product of Hollywood

I see God's image
in every person
an intrinsic value
This is God's assertion

I see God's promises
Coming to pass!
So trust in the Lord
to Him hold fast!

I Am Joy

And do not be grieved, for the
joy of the LORD is your strength.
(Nehemiah 8:10 ESV)

God's joy is fuel for our lives. When you are low on this fuel, rejoice in the Lord! This is what Paul and Silas did when they were in the Philippians jail. It caused an earthquake and brought their release from prison. That's the power of God's joy!

Lord, fill us up again with Your joy that we may have the strength to live our lives fully for Your glory!

I am Joy
Feel my strength
My power takes you
to any length

I am here
in the midst of sadness
Not just present
in times of gladness

My source is in
the being of God
Over you, I smile
Over you, I applaud

The Lord Jesus
fully displayed
The heart of joy
He conveyed

I am Joy
Rejoice in me
Come to know
My delight and glee!

I am Grace

For the grace of God has been
revealed, bringing salvation
to all people. (Titus 2:11 NLT)

Amazing grace how sweet the sound! God's grace is truly amazing! This grace is not just a concept to know in our heads, but a living reality to be experienced. Today! Grace is so much more than the forgiveness of sins. Grace includes the power and resources from heaven that we need to live the abundant life of Christ. Receive His grace afresh!

Lord, thank You for Your grace. I receive it afresh today. I receive Your power and strength from above to live as more than a conqueror in Jesus!

I am Grace
Freely receive
No need to earn
Just believe

Unmerited favor
Poured from above
The heart of the Father
His agape love

Mercy is
Judgment suspended
I am
Abundance extended

Not just forgiveness
but the power to live
See all the ways
that I can give

I am Grace
Unlimited supply
Meant for today
Not pie in the sky!

I Am Weakness

> For my weakness becomes a portal to God's power. (2 Corinthians 12:10 TPT)

The ways of the Kingdom are opposite from the ways of the world. In the world, weakness pounced upon and despised. So weakness is to be avoided at all costs.

Weakness is strength in the Kingdom God! Our weakness becomes the very place where we experience God's strength and power.

Today, let's lean into our weakness, not turn away from it. Let's draw on the immeasurable strength and power from God that flows into our weakness!

I am Weakness
I reside
in every person
Don't try to hide

When you acknowledge
me you find
A whole new strength
the heavenly kind

I am power
in disguise
Glory in me
and your pride dies

Weakness shines
for all to see
The beauty of
vulnerability

I am Weakness
Here I am
When you can't
then you can!

I Am Lament

> I hurt with the hurt of my people.
> I mourn and am overcome with
> grief. (Jeremiah 8:21 NLT)

We need to release the deep pains and hurts that we have been harboring in our hearts. When we hold it in, our hearts are weighed down. The Lord calls us to release our hearts in lament to Him.

Lord, I am hurting! Lord, I am in pain! I need Your comfort and Your relief. I need You to let me know that I will be okay. I trust that You are making all things for the good for I love You and have been called according to Your purpose.

I am Lament
Hear my cry
When you're in pain
do not deny

or suppress
Give me release
a crucial step
on your way to peace

How long, O Lord
must we wait
Endless pandemic
Will it abate?

I trust in You, Lord
In the midst
of my suffering
I will persist

I find relief
in knowing
That God is with me
in the rough going!

I Am Shame

Shame came into the world and into our lives as a result of the fall. Adam and Eve were without sin and felt no shame. After they sinned, they felt shame. Shame is more about who we are than what we do. We feel like we are worthless, not good enough. Jesus took our shame upon Himself when He went to the cross on our behalf.

He sets us free from our shame! Praise God!

Lord, thank You for taking my shame upon the Cross. Release me from my shame. Fill me afresh with Your unconditional love. Help me to know that I am accepted and that You see me as precious and worthy of Your love.

I am Shame
You know my name
Because of me
you love to blame

I dwell deeply
in people's souls
I am a great big
gaping hole

Of pain and self-hate
Worthlessness
I am the cause
of emptiness

When Jesus died
upon the cross
He despised the shame
He paid the cost

To see you free
from my grip
To live now as
His workmanship!

I Am Rejection

When my father and my mother forsake me, Then the Lord will take care of me. (Psalm 27:10 NKJV)

Rejection is one of the most painful human experiences there is. We experience rejection from many different sources- from our parents, friends, and strangers. One of the most painful forms of rejection is self-rejection. God can heal the wounds we have received from rejection. His acceptance and love are the cure. As we fully embrace His acceptance of us as His children, the wounds of rejection are healed!

Lord, I am fully accepted by You! Heal me from the wounds I have received from being rejected by others. Heal me of self- rejection. I accept myself because You have loved and accepted me!

I am Rejection
I'm filled with shame
So many people
feel my pain

I am hurt
when you don't press "like"
When I get triggered
it's fight or flight

Longing for love
Gasping for air
Childhood wounds
that are still there

Almost impossible
to soothe my pain
I'm the reason for addiction
time and again

Who can relieve
The pain I'm feeling?
Only God's love
can bring my healing!

Chapter 5

Spiritual Warfare Poems

The Bible tells us that we are all in a continual spiritual battle. This is part of the biblical worldview. The devil and his forces are real. The good news is that Jesus completely defeated the devil through His victory on the cross! As believers in Jesus, we share in this victory! Therefore, we fight from victory, not for victory. May these poems on spiritual warfare help you experience this victory!

Break Every Chain!

> It shall come to pass in that day
> That his burden will be taken away
> from your shoulder, And his yoke
> from your neck, And the yoke
> will be destroyed because of the
> anointing oil. (Isaiah 10:27 NKJV)

The spiritual battle is real! We have an adversary that seeks to bring havoc in our lives. The Good News is that Jesus has defeated the enemy on the cross! His disciples are to live the Lord's victory.

The Lord breaks every chain that hinders our lives! There is power in the Name of Jesus. He gives us His authority over all the forces of evil. We are called to exercise that authority that we have been given in His Name. No weapon formed against us will prosper!

There's power in His name
to break every chain
All authority is His
The King of Kings, He reigns!

Depression has no place
Sickness must go
By His stripes, we're healed
Darkness overthrow

The name above all names
Jesus Christ, the Lord
The victory is won!
His Word is our sword

Speak the name of Jesus
Release His power now
At the name of Jesus
every knee shall bow

Every tongue confess
The glory of His name
By faith, we proclaim
He's breaking every chain!

The Battle Belongs to the Lord

> And everyone assembled here
> will know that the LORD rescues
> his people, but not with sword
> and spear. This is the LORD's
> battle, and he will give you
> to us! (1 Samuel 17:47 NLT)

The battle belongs to the Lord! When David faced Goliath, he knew he was fighting a spiritual battle and that the Lord was on his side. He knew that with God's power that Goliath was going down!

The Lord is fighting on our behalf, bringing us the victory in His Name. We do not need to fear, for the Lord is near! He has already won the victory on the Cross. Live in the Victory of Jesus!

Facing Goliath
with his stones and sling
David ran to the battle
His soul began to sing

"This battle belongs
to the Lord
He is my shield
He is my sword

"In the Lord's name
You will fall
God will answer
when I call"

He swung the slingshot
Hit the mark
Goliath's world
soon got dark

Whatever battle
you face today
Fight with faith
and win His way!

Worry or Worship?

> But the Lord said to her, "My dear Martha, you are worried and upset over all these details! There is only one thing worth being concerned about. Mary has discovered it, and it will not be taken away from her." (Luke 10:41–42 NLT)

There are so many things that we face in life that cause worry. The Lord tells us not to worry, to trust in Him. He is in control of our lives. We need not worry! Instead of worrying, we just need to worship! When we worry, our problems get amplified. When we worship, our problems shrink in the light of the greatness of our God. Let's make the choice today to worship instead of worry.

Worry or worship?
Which will it be?
Worship the Lord!
Your soul is set free

Worry says, "I am
The one in control
In my world
I play the title role"

Worship says, "He
Rules and reigns on high
I stand in awe
on Him, I rely"

Worry weighs down
Worship lifts up
Worry brings low
Worship fills your cup!

Worry or worship?
Come make your choice
As for me and my house
We will rejoice!

Be Strong and Courageous!

> This is my command—be strong
> and courageous! Do not be afraid
> or discouraged. For the LORD
> your God is with you wherever
> you go. (Joshua 1:9 NLT)

Joshua faced an extremely challenging task, leading the people of Israel into the Promised Land. He had to fill the shoes of Moses, Israel's greatest leader. The Lord encouraged Joshua to be the leader that He was calling him to be.

Brothers and sisters, be strong and courageous! The Lord is with you! As you take hold of the promised land that He has for you, know that the Lord goes before you and will help you overcome every obstacle you face. His Presence gives you strength and courage to fight the battle and win!

Be strong and courageous!
Don't give way to fear
for I am with you
I am always near

When you go to battle
rely upon My power
Jericho's walls will fall
I am your strong tower

As I was with Moses
so I'll be with you
Just be yourself
No need to fill his shoes

I will go before you
Fighting on your behalf
My promises are true
signed with My autograph

Be strong and courageous
The victory is yours!
I know how it ends
I know the final score!

Spirit of Might

> I also pray that you will understand the incredible greatness of God's power for us who believe him. This is the same mighty power that raised Christ from the dead and seated him in the place of honor at God's right hand in the heavenly realms. (Ephesians 1:19–20 NLT)

The Spirit of Might lives in us! The same power that raised Jesus from the dead gives us the strength we need to live victorious lives. The Spirit of Might will empower you in every thing you do. Miracles and breakthroughs will happen in Jesus' Mighty Name. We can overcome the works of darkness in His mighty power. May we rely upon His Spirit today and do the impossible! Hallelujah!

Spirit of Might
move in our midst
How we need You
to assist!

Shake the earth
and shake our hearts
Break the status quo
fully apart!

Heal the sick
through our prayers
Showing the world
that You care

Power that raised
Jesus from the dead
lives inside us
Full steam ahead!

Spirit of Might!
Come ignite
our hearts on fire
Heaven's dynamite!

Songs of Freedom

> Now the Lord is the Spirit, and where the Spirit of the Lord is, there is freedom. (2 Corinthians 3:17 NIV)

There is freedom in the Lord! We have been set free by what Jesus did for us on the cross. Sing of His Freedom! Sing because He has set you free! Free from fear! Free from condemnation! Free to be all that God has called you to be. Live in the freedom that Jesus purchased for you. Hallelujah!

Songs of freedom
I will sing
With all my heart
worshipping

The Lord is good
He set me free
In my trouble
He heard my plea

I'll declare
My testimony
Tell the world
my salvation story

On the cross
He ransomed me
Paid my debt
on the tree

Hear the songs
and join the chorus
God is with us
He is for us!

By My Spirit

Greater is the One in us than the one in the world. The enemy has been defeated! Rely upon His power to overcome every tactic and scheme of the adversary. We have supernatural strength and power available to us by His Spirit. We are more than conquerors in and through Jesus!

Not by power
Nor by might
But by My Spirit
you shall fight!

When you face
the raging foe
Look to Me
I will bestow

Faith and strength
to win the battle
Nothing ever
Gets Me rattled

Jehovah Nissi
is My name
Raise My banner
by faith proclaim

"The victory
is the Lord's!"
I am your shield
your great reward!

Civilian Affairs

> No one serving as a soldier
> gets entangled in civilian
> affairs, but rather tries to
> please his commanding
> officer. (2 Timothy 2:4 NIV)

Civilian affairs are the pressing things in our lives that we need to attend to each day. They can bog us down in the spiritual battle. We are called to engage in the battle each and every day with Jesus as our Commander in Chief. We are in God's army! May we not get distracted by civilian affairs.Let us be whole focused and engaged in fighting the good fight.

May I not get entangled
in civilian affairs
Won't be weighed down
with this world's cares

To fight the good fight
To finish my race
Lay hold of the prize
It's all by Your grace

May my heart not be divided
May my focus be clear
When the Lord speaks
may I always give ear

I'm in His army
a Kingdom soldier
In the day of battle
may I keep my composure

To heed His command
To hear His "well done!"
Living before
an audience of One!

My Trust Declaration

> Some trust in chariots and some in horses, but we trust in the name of the LORD our God. (Psalm 20:7 NIV)

Make a fresh trust declaration today. I put my trust in the Lord, not in anything else! Nothing else can compare to the Lord! The Lord is worthy of my trust, as He has proven reliable again and again. He is faithful to keep His promises with His people. The Lord never fails!

I put my trust in You
for all the world to see
In these troubled times
You're my security

The rock on which I stand
All other ground will sink
New crises come by the day
Things change in a blink

I will not trust my feelings
I will not trust my eyes
I will trust in You
The God who is all wise

You rule and reign on high
You care for the weak
You will never leave us
especially when things are bleak

All who trust in You
are never put to shame
Lord, we trust in You
We praise Your holy name!

Worship Warrior

Worship is a powerful weapon! The Bible shows us that our worship is a spiritual weapon to defeat the forces of darkness. When we worship the Lord, God dwells in our praises and moves in power in our midst. Worship declares the greatness of our God, inviting Him in real time to bring us His victory!

I am a worship warrior
David is my name
Winning spiritual battles
Praising is my game

My weapons are my songs
sung to God Most High
Lifting the name of Jesus
The shout is my war cry

God dwells in our praises
His presence can be felt
When we praise name
the enemy is dealt

a big defeating blow
The devil cannot stand
His weapons are disarmed
He's overplayed his hand

Come join the army
Worship warriors unite
We fight not flesh and blood
in this spiritual fight!

Six Steps

> After the men who were carrying
> the Ark of the Lord had gone six
> steps, David sacrificed a bull and a
> fattened calf. (2 Samuel 6:13 NLT)

A sacrifice every six steps! As David brought in the Ark into Jerusalem, he meticulously followed the prescribed order of worship. Our God is a God of order.

In the New Testament, God calls us to worship Him in Spirit and in truth. Believers are called to offer a sacrifice of praise (praising God in the midst of difficulties) and to present our lives as living sacrifices to the Lord. As we do, the Lord receives our praise and is glorified in and through our lives.

Walk six steps
then sacrifice
David's plan
The costly price

I will not offer
Praise that's cheap
Will cost you everything
The price is steep

To fear the Lord
Obey His ways
To shout for joy
His banner raise

Dancing jumping
Undignified
Killing all
my foolish pride

Lord You're worthy
of all my praise
In every moment
not just Sundays!

Chapter 6

Be Like Jesus Poems

The goal of every disciple of Jesus is to be like Jesus, our Lord and teacher. These poems take different qualities of the Lord and encourage the disciple to follow in His footsteps.

Serve like Jesus

> For even the Son of Man came not
> to be served but to serve others
> and to give his life as a ransom
> for many. (Mark 10:45 NLT)

Jesus is a Servant! He is God, yet He came not to be served but to serve! In our Lord Jesus, we have an example and model for us to follow. He washed the dirty feet of His disciples; He calls us to do the same. As we serve others, we are becoming like our Master.

How can we serve others today? Take some time to ask the Lord for how specifically He is calling you to serve others. Just do it!

Help me, Lord
to serve like Jesus
No longer wanting others
to always please us

Take up the towel
and wash dirty feet
Not just once
but willing to repeat

To care for others
for those in need
Overcoming
my selfish greed

To give is better
than to receive
To serve is better
than to achieve

Jesus, help me
serve like You
To a hurting world
may You shine through!

Smell like Jesus

> Our lives are a Christ-like
> fragrance rising up to God.
> But this fragrance is perceived
> differently by those who are being
> saved and by those who are
> perishing. (2 Corinthians 2:15 NLT)

There is an aroma that exudes from our lives when we walk in close communion with Jesus. It is the aroma of Jesus. Jesus' life exuded the aroma of love and joy. This is what the world needs today! There is the stench of hatred, division, and hopelessness permeating our atmosphere. As followers of Jesus, may His aroma be like a sweet smelling incense that changes what our world smells like!

Help me, Lord
to smell like Jesus
Fresh fragrance
from heaven fill us!

Aroma of Christ
fills the air
Emanating
Everywhere

His people are
They smell like Him
Holy sweat
from the Kingdom gym

The smell of joy
and love and peace
Enticing us
to heaven's feast

In this world
of toxic fumes
May the smell of Jesus
fill earth's rooms!

Dying with Jesus

> My old self has been crucified with Christ. It is no longer I who live, but Christ lives in me. So I live in this earthly body by trusting in the Son of God, who loved me and gave himself for me. (Galatians 2:20 NLT)

The Lord calls me to take up my cross daily- to die to my fleshly and selfish desires. This is the call of the Christian. We are to follow in the footsteps of our Lord, who gladly went to the Cross on our behalf. So often we want resurrection, but we need to die to self first and then experience His resurrection in our lives.

Taking up my cross
to follow You
Dying to self
Rising anew

Die to the flesh
and selfish gain
Break my heart
with what brings You pain

Die to the world
and all its schemes
Living for
the Kingdom team

We want the crown
without the cross
Doing everything
to avoid loss

We hear the call
To die with You
Life eternal
Breaking through!

Heal like Jesus

> I tell you the truth, anyone who believes in me will do the same works I have done, and even greater works, because I am going to be with the Father. (John 14:12 NLT)

Healing was a very big part of Jesus' ministry while He walked the earth. He had great compassion upon those who were suffering and healed people of their physical ailments and diseases. Jesus said His followers would do the same things He did, even greater things! Can it be true? Yes, it is! In the book of Acts, His followers healed people in Jesus' Name. We are called to lay hands upon the sick today and see them healed in Jesus' Name!

To heal like Jesus
is my call
In His name
make the withdrawal

Of heaven's healing
He said we could
His disciples
if only they would

Lay their hands
in faith and pray
We'd see miracles
this very day

Jesus is the same
Today and tomorrow
It's His authority
that we borrow

Lord, bring healing
In Your name
In this world
Increase Your fame!

Think like Jesus

> Don't copy the behavior and
> customs of this world, but let God
> transform you into a new person by
> changing the way you think. Then
> you will learn to know God's will for
> you, which is good and pleasing
> and perfect. (Romans 12:2 NLT)

Jesus' thinking was in alignment with the Kingdom of God. He was not limited by what He saw in the natural world; He was able to see and draw from the supernatural dimension of the Kingdom.

I want to think like Jesus! I want to have the mind of Christ, seeing people and situations from the heavenly point of view. Human thinking is so limited and confining. Jesus sees problems as opportunities for breakthrough. Yes and amen!

Help me, Lord
to think like Jesus
The mind of Christ
bequeathed to us

To see from heaven's
Point of view
The world's lies
seeing through

Abundance mindset
I can do all things
through Christ whose strength
gives me wings

Seeing problems
with God in mind
Leaving doubt
Unbelief behind

To think like Jesus
A faith-filled mind
All things are possible
I'm unconfined!

Rise with Jesus

Sharing in his death by our baptism means that we were co-buried with him, so that when the Father's glory raised Christ from the dead, we were also raised with him. We have been co-resurrected with him so that we could be empowered to walk in the freshness of new life. (Romans 6:4 TPT)

I am Risen with Christ, living in His Resurrection power! The amount of power that we have available to us through the Holy Spirit is truly mind blowing. We need to access this power through faith.

Lord, help us to lay hold of the power that is living in us. This power helps us overcome our sinful nature. This power also flows through us to bring healing to others. The same power that raised Jesus from the dead is living in me! I can do all things through Christ who gives me strength! I am more than a conqueror in Christ!

On the third day
Jesus rose again
Bringing life
to all His friends

Because He lives
We too shall live
The Resurrection
Determinative

Of our future
It is secure
Our home in heaven
our place is sure

Rise with Jesus
here and now
To live your life
He'll show you how

Risen with Jesus
I'm born again
Let the redeemed
Say amen!

Love like Jesus

> Dear friends, let us love one another, for love comes from God. Everyone who loves has been born of God and knows God. (1 John 4:7 NIV)

Jesus' followers are to be known by their love. The love of Jesus first flows to our lives, then flows from our lives to others.

I want to love like Jesus! Greater love has none than this, that a man lays down his life for His friends. Following Jesus, I want to lay down my life for others. I want to tangibly demonstrate Christ's love to others through my words and my deeds!

Help me, Lord
to love like Jesus
Loving others
is what frees us

Washing feet
Helping the poor
Demonstrating
God's amor

Showing empathy
for others' pain
Loving those
who show disdain

Dying to self
Taking up my cross
Being His disciple
There is a cost

To love like Jesus
is my desire
Turn my spark
into a fire!

Look like Jesus

> And consider the example that
> Jesus, the Anointed One, has
> set before us. Let his mindset
> become your motivation.
> (Philippians 2:5 TPT)

When people see my life, may they see Jesus! Followers of Jesus are called to look like Him. We are being transformed daily into His likeness. He removes the things in our lives that don't resemble Him. He helps us develop the fruit of the Spirit in our lives. He is the source of my life and my reason for existence. As I follow and imitate Him, I pray that I may resemble His likeness to a watching and hurting world.

Lord, I want to
look like Jesus
To see myself
as You see us

Not the picture
on the wall
But with actions
big and small

The *imago Dei*
that lives in me
Let my light shine
for all to see

When people see me
May they see You
May I be a sign
pointing to

the One who saves
Jesus the Christ
Who gives to all
Abundant life!

More like Jesus

> But the fruit produced by the Holy Spirit within you is divine love in all its varied expressions: joy that overflows, peace that subdues, patience that endures, kindness in action, a life full of virtue, faith that prevails, gentleness of heart, and strength of spirit. Never set the law above these qualities, for they are meant to be limitless. (Galatians 5:22–23, TPT)

I want to be more like Jesus! We have come a long way; we have a long way to go. It is a lifelong journey.

Lord, daily change me more and more into Your Likeness! Help me to reflect the same fruit of the Spirit that was so beautifully displayed in Your life. Don't stop changing me until I see You face to face!

I want to be
more like Jesus
This is the life
that truly frees us

A life of humility
A life filled with love
A life to the full
What a disciple's made of

Less of me
Less of my pride
Less of the world
Less trying to hide

More of Jesus
More of His grace
More of His power
More seeking His face

More like Jesus
This is my prayer!
Living in the Kingdom
under His care!

Chapter 7

Renewal Poems

In the day-to-day grind of life, we can lose our strength and spiritual vitality. The Lord comes to us in fresh ways and brings spiritual renewal into our lives. Those who wait upon the Lord will renew their strength (Isaiah 40:31). These poems on renewal are meant to be a catalyst for spiritual renewal in your life. Be renewed in the Lord!

More than I Can Ask or Imagine

> Now to him who is able to do immeasurably more than all we ask or imagine, according to his power that is at work within us. (Ephesians 3:20 NIV)

Our God can do more than we ask or imagine! Think about this reality for a few minutes today. God can accomplish our greatest request and can fulfill our biggest dream. For real? Yes! Our God is Almighty and All powerful! Our problems are small from His perspective. When we put our trust in our awesome God, we will see Him work miracles in our lives!

More than I can ask
or even imagine
You can do more, Lord
You can make it happen!

So much bigger
than what I can think
Expand my mind
My thoughts are rinky-dink

Break out of the box
inside my head
Taking away the doubts
Fill it with faith instead!

God of the universe
Over all You reign
All the galaxies
under Your domain

Be still and know that You are God
You're fully in control
You reign eternally
No need to take a poll!

Awaken the Dawn

> Awake, my soul! Awake, harp and lyre! I will awaken the dawn. (Psalm 57:8 NIV)

So often in life we face dark times. Hope runs thin and our faith falters. What is the way out of the darkness? Praise!! I will awaken the dawn with my praises to the Lord! When darkness surrounds me, I will not fear, for the Lord is with me. In the midst of trials, I will praise the Lord who will come to my rescue. My praises welcome His Presence into my life and circumstances. In His Presence, the walls of Jericho come tumbling down!

Night is ending
Morning has come
I will awaken the dawn
Here comes the sun!

Evening to morning
Mourning to dancing
Breaking the dawn
Your Kingdom's advancing

Life's so hard
in the middle of the trial
Make me like Jesus
It's all worthwhile

Sacrifice of praise
bringing me through
Leading me to
Your point of view

I will awaken the dawn
Breakthrough is here!
He's overcome the world
Be of good cheer!

The Fiery Furnace

"Look!" Nebuchadnezzar shouted.
"I see four men, unbound,
walking around in the fire
unharmed! And the fourth looks
like a god!" (Daniel 3:25 NLT)

God is with us in the fiery furnace! The furnace is the place where our faith is tested and God comes through in a big way. As He was with Shadrach, Meschach, and Abednego in the furnace, so he is with us! It is especially in the midst of trials that we experience God in real and powerful ways. He is there to protect, comfort, and strengthen us in our difficult times. If you are facing a difficult trial today, take comfort in His Presence.

When I'm in
The fiery furnace
I am scared
I must confess

How could God
Lead me here
Is He there?
Did He disappear?

Wake up my soul
and see Him near
He is there
Be of good cheer

He will guide me
through this trial
In the end
It'll be worthwhile

For the furnace
forms Christ in me
Pain God's megaphone
Often necessary!

The Quiet Hour

Encounter the Lord in the quiet hour of the morning! A new day begins with His new mercies poured out on your life. He longs to have fellowship with you, to meet you in a powerful way. He gives us our daily manna to nourish our souls. Fellowship with the Lord in the morning is so sweet; it prepares for the rest of the day.

The quiet hour
My time with You
The world is sleeping
as the morning dew

Forms on the ground
I hear the sounds
Your gentle whispers
all around

All the noise
and all the clutter
I can hear my heart
It starts to flutter

Perfect peace
and clarity
Holy communion
Intimacy

The quiet hour
My favorite time
I am Yours
and You are mine.

Waterfall

> Deep calls to deep in the roar
> of your waterfalls; all your waves
> and breakers have swept
> over me. (Psalm 42:7 NIV)

The waterfall is a wonderful picture of spiritual refreshing from the Lord. The Holy Spirit being poured out upon us. Live under the waterfall of His Presence! Be refreshed! Be renewed! Be engulfed in His goodness! His unfailing love is truly like a powerful waterfall, pouring over our souls bringing cleansing and renewal to our lives.

Living water waterfall
Shower down on me
Cleansing and refreshing
Oh so lovingly

Healing stream of life
making my heart whole
Treating my deep wounds
Restoring my soul

Breathing fresh new life
to places that have died
Bringing resurrection
to what's been crucified

My great big thirst cannot be quenched
by the things of man
Only You, Lord, fill me up
in a way no other can

Holy Spirit waterfall
I plunge into You
Losing self to find it
Old life, I bid adieu!

Kairos Time

> For if you remain completely silent at this time, relief and deliverance will arise for the Jews from another place, but you and your father's house will perish. Yet who knows whether you have come to the kingdom for *such* a time as this? (Esther 4:14 NKJV)

We are living in a Kairos Time! God raised up Esther to do mighty things for the Kingdom. He strategically placed Esther in a position of influence as queen to bring about deliverance for God's people.

He has raised you up in this time to do great things for His Kingdom too! The Lord has placed you right where you are for strategic Kingdom influence. Take hold of the calling that is upon your life. Courageously step into what God has opened for you. He has raised you up for such a time as this!

This is kairos time!
Where God is on the move
He's working all around
Get into His groove!

For such a time as this
God has raised us up!
To be the salt and light
To overflow our cups

Into the world we live
This time of fear and pain
To spread His perfect peace
To extend His rule and reign

Like Esther in the Bible
Bold and without fear
Standing before the king
Changing the atmosphere

Kairos time is now!
God's appointed hour
Holy Spirit, come
move in might and power!

Recharge

> Revive us again, O God! I know you will! Give us a fresh start! Then all your people will taste your joy and gladness. (Psalm 85:6 TPT)

Recharge our souls, Lord! How we need your fresh touch! Living in this world, our souls get weary and tired. The spiritual battle rages on each and every day. Come breathe Your fresh power into our soul socket. The same power that raised Jesus from the dead is living in me! Thank you, Lord, for recharging me today!

Oh, how we need
A full life recharge!
The problems we've been facing
are size extra large!

Covid's still a problem
The world won't be the same
He's still in control
The name above all names

Help us to plug in
to the power source above
Take in His resurrection
Take in His agape love

Finding strength in You
We feel Your life within
Feeling fresh vitality
where we've been wearing thin

Recharging taking place
Our tank has been refilled!
Now we are ready
to take the next hill!

Heart on Fire

> But if I say I'll never mention the
> LORD or speak in his name, his
> word burns in my heart like a
> fire. It's like a fire in my bones! I
> am worn out trying to hold it in! I
> can't do it! (Jeremiah 20:9 NLT)

God calls us to live with hearts on fire for Him! He tells us that lukewarm won't do (Revelation 3:20). This heart on fire comes from knowing that God is passionately in love with us!

Give me a heart on fire for You, Lord! I want to be on fire for the Kingdom! May the same fire that burned in Jeremiah burn in me. Burn away the dross on my soul. I want to live a life filled with passion and that is all out for You!

Give me, Lord
a heart on fire
Passion growing
Burning desire

A burning bush
may my heart be
Roaring flame
for all to see

Burn away
All of the dross
Flesh crucified
on the cross

Living sacrifice
to You I bring
Fire consuming
Everything

Give me, Lord
A heart on Fire
Raging, growing
Flames going higher!

Hope Is Rising

> And this hope will not lead to disappointment. For we know how dearly God loves us, because he has given us the Holy Spirit to fill our hearts with his love. (Romans 5:5 NLT)

Hope is rising! God's hope does not disappoint us. Worldly hope will surely let us down. We have a God who is all powerful and all loving and He is for us and not against us. Therefore, we never lose hope for this God is always with us. Grab hold of the hope that comes from knowing the God of hope today!

Hope is rising
in the air
God is working
everywhere

Birds are singing
Chirps of praise
Feel the warmth
of the sun's rays

Winter snow
Melting away
Flowers blooming
Full array

Hope is stirring
in our hearts
Getting ready
New season starts

God is moving
in this hour
Hope is real
Feel its power!

Break of Dawn

Early in the morning will I seek You, Lord! In the morning hour, while the world sleeps, You and I enjoy sweet fellowship together. You download the secrets of Your heart to my heart. You pour in the fresh resources of the Kingdom into my being. I am ready for the new day!

The break of dawn
My favorite time
Light breaking in
The birds start to chime

Things getting brighter
The new day begins
The Kingdom of God
now breaking in

Sweet hour of worship
Sweet hour of prayer
Time to lie down
All to His care

No distractions
None of the noise
Setting aside
The world and its toys

Break of dawn's here!
Every day
The pillar of fire
leading the way!

Times of Refreshing

> Repent therefore and be
> converted, that your sins
> may be blotted out, so that
> times of refreshing may come
> from the presence of the
> Lord. (Acts 3:19 NKJV)

Bring times of refreshing, Lord! Showers of power, showers of love pouring over my soul. In Your Presence, there is fullness of joy. Just spending a few minutes in Your Presence face to face brings refreshing to my soul!

How I need
times of refreshing!
Poured from on high
showers of blessing

May the living water
refresh my soul
I lay down my burdens
I release control

This life leaves me weary
Battered and worn
I am His sheep
My pride has been shorn

Perfect place to be
to receive His grace
He's near to the broken
will always embrace

Filling me up
I feel the river
Times of refreshing
You always deliver!

Sweetly Broken

> My sacrifice, O God, is a broken spirit; a broken and contrite heart you, God, will not despise. (Psalm 51:17 NIV)

I am sweetly broken by Your love! When I encounter Your love in a fresh way, my pride melts away. Your kindness leads me to repentance. In my place of brokenness I find Your healing. In my weakness, I find Your strength. There's no place I'd rather be!

I've been sweetly broken
by Your love
Surrendered to
the gentle Dove

Learning of
my limitations
Leads me into
activation

From my strength
to Your might
Being set free
from this dogfight

Like Jacob wrestling
all night with You
I have a new name
from my breakthrough

Loved by God
that's all that matters
My life's now filled
with holy laughter!

Shalom

I live in Your Shalom, Lord! A place of rest, a place of peace. A place of safety from my enemies. Well being of body, soul, and mind. Harmony with my neighbors. Peace with my enemies. Your Shalom is the best place to live!

Shalom
My home
With God
Peace zone

Well-being
of soul
My life
made whole

In Him
find rest
In God
so blessed

Protects heart
and mind
Totally
aligned

Shalom
is here
Gone is
all fear!

Heaven's Breeze

> Suddenly a sound like the blowing of a violent wind came from heaven and filled the whole house where they were sitting. (Acts 2:2 NIV)

Heaven's breeze changes the atmosphere! Heaven invading the earth, bringing change and transformation. Heaven breathing life into the dry bones of lost people. Heaven invading my life, stirring up the gifts that lay dormant, empowering me to live my best life for God!

Heaven's breeze
blows o'er my soul
Releasing me
from things that troll

Peace descending
into my heart
Holy Spirit
You impart

Gentle whisper
Soothing sounds
I hear Your voice
in You, I'm found

Freed from worry
Freed from fear
Free to be
True self appears

Enjoy the moment
Heaven come
A little taste
We've just begun!

New Wine

How we long to drink Your New Wine, Lord! The new wine
of joy in this dreary world. The new wine of hope in these
despairing times we are living in. Just as You transformed
the water into wine at the wedding in Cana, transform
the water of our lives into Your New wine!

Pour out the new wine!
The wine of Your Spirit
When You speak
help me to hear it

More of Your joy
More of Your peace
Dining at Your table
in a continual feast!

Be filled with the Spirit
Be not drunk with wine
Tastes so much better
This wine from the vine!

Communing with Jesus
Enjoying His presence
Living with His
total acceptance

All can enjoy
This new wine is blessed
There is no hangover
This wine is the best!

New Wineskins

And no one puts new wine into old wineskins; or else the new wine bursts the wineskins, the wine is spilled, and the wineskins are ruined. But new wine must be put into new wineskins. (Mark 2:22 NKJV)

We need new wineskins to contain the new wine that You have for us, Lord! The old wineskins of our traditions must be shed. Stale faith and the desire to preserve the status quo must be shed too. Give us a fresh heart of worship and faith, Lord. These are the new wineskins needed today.

New wine needs
New wineskins!
A new container
to put the wine in!

The character of Jesus
The fruits of love
Joy and peace
flowing from above

A new attitude
A heart filled with praise
This is the new wineskin
A life that's ablaze

with spiritual passion
Zeal for the lost
The life of discipleship
counting the cost

New wineskin is ready!
Pour in new wine
Say to the world
"Come and dine!"

Recommissioned

> But you will receive power
> when the Holy Spirit comes
> upon you. And you will be
> my witnesses, telling people
> about me everywhere—in
> Jerusalem, throughout Judea,
> in Samaria, and to the ends
> of the earth. (Acts 1:8 NLT)

The Lord is recommissioning us for His mission—the Great Commission! The same calling upon the original disciples is upon Jesus's disciples today. We have been called to make disciples of all nations, baptizing them and teaching them to obey everything Jesus commanded. There is no greater cause worth living for!

Volcano erupting
fresh within my soul
Releasing all the pain
Releasing all control

Crying out to Jesus
The only One who saves
He endured the cross
He overcame the grave

Resurrection power
Surging through my veins
Giving me the strength
to run in my lane

Fresh recommissioning
Jesus tells us, "Go!
Make disciples of all
Let all people know

"That I am coming soon
I'll make all things right
until that glorious day
Fight the good fight!

Chapter 8

Places Poems

There are different places where we can encounter the Lord in fresh ways. Our God is a god of variety and adventure. Encounter the Lord in a powerful way in these places!

Resting Place

Arise, LORD, and come to your resting place, you and the ark of your might. (Psalm 132:8 NIV)

How we need a Resting Place! A place where we can exhale, unwind, and find rest. Our Lord Jesus is our Resting Place! He tells us to come to Him and find rest in Him. His yoke is easy and His burden is light. Find rest in Him today!

Lord, You are
My resting place
Where I can heal
My true home base

Release my burdens
My soul needs rest
Let down my guard
and decompress

Perfect peace
In You, there's solace
Tender Shepherd
By name, You call us

A place where I
am fully known
Am fully loved
Am called Your own

Breathing in
Your love and grace
Blessed Holy
Interface!

Hiding Place

> You are my hiding place; you
> will protect me from trouble
> and surround me with songs of
> deliverance. (Psalm 32:7 NIV)

The Lord is our Hiding Place! The place where we can find shelter from the attack of the enemy. The safe place where we can bring our shame and our pain and find shelter, healing, and protection. We can recharge our spirits as we spend time in the Hiding Place.

The battle rages
every day
I need a respite
from the fray

The hiding place
The place I find
Where my heart
is realigned

Take a breather
from the fight
Take some time
to delight

In Your goodness
Your loving care
Jehovah Shammah
You are there

O hiding place
Here I come!
The strengthening
has begun!

The Secret Place

> When we live our lives within
> the shadow of God Most High,
> our secret hiding place, we
> will always be shielded from
> harm. How then could evil
> prevail against us or disease
> infect us? (Psalm 91:9–10 TPT)

God has reserved a Secret Place just for you. A place where you can intimately commune with Him. A place where You can hear Him tenderly speak to you and where you can pour out your heart to Him. Look for your secret place with God- here you will find all that you need!

The secret place
is where I find
Refuge and comfort
Peace of mind

A place to rest
A place to chill
A place to play
A place to fill

My heart with You
My loving Lord
Where we can be
in one accord

Where I find shelter
from the storm
Loved unconditionally
No need to perform

The secret place
My favorite space
where I meet You
Face-to-face!

The Waiting Room

> Wait patiently for the LORD.
> Be brave and courageous.
> Yes, wait patiently for the
> LORD. (Psalm 27:14 NLT)

Come to the Waiting Room and find the best company you will ever know! The Lord Himself will meet you in the waiting room and will wait with you as you go through the trials and difficulties of life. In the Waiting Room, we are transformed more into the likeness of Jesus and we develop a deeper intimacy with Him.

Who likes to wait?
No, not me!
Waiting is so hard
can I do it absentee?

I've found the secret!
It's waiting on the Lord
It's the perfect time
to get into accord

It's waiting WITH the Lord
He'll keep you company
Wooing with His kindness
loving tenderly

Then you realize
Waiting can be good!
In the waiting room
In Jesus' neighborhood

Waiting is the time
when we can grow our trust
For growing in our character
waiting is a must!

Heaven Come!

> Your kingdom come. Your will be done On earth as it is in heaven. (Matthew 6:10 NKJV)

Let Heaven Come down here on earth today! The joy of heaven, the peace of heaven, the power of Heaven. These are all available here and now. Ask and you will receive. Ask our Heavenly Father to pour down the blessings of heaven into your life and world today!

Future Kingdom
is at hand
Heaven come
into our land

The King is here
He rules and reigns
The light enters
Darkness wanes

Taste and see
That He is good
Experience
His Fatherhood

Power and
Authority
His Kingdom is
reality

Heaven come!
Your will be done!
Winning souls
one by one!

The Wilderness

> But He made His own people go forth like sheep, And guided them in the wilderness like a flock. (Psalm 78:52 NKJV)

The Lord is faithful to lead us through the Wilderness! The wilderness is a place where we can feel lost. Confused. Wandering. It is in the wilderness where we learn to trust God in a deeper way. It is a place where we learn to follow Him one day at a time. God is surely with us in the wilderness!

Lead me through
the wilderness
Let me know
Your tenderness

Trusting You
wholeheartedly
For You already
parted the sea

Daily manna
My provision
Just enough
This is Your wisdom

Keep my heart
In the wilderness
Keep my soul
from bitterness

Promised land
Here I come!
O wilderness
please soon be done!

Place of Refuge

The Lord is our refuge and our fortress! When the storms
of life come, where can we go? To Whom can we go?
To the place of refuge, the Lord Jesus Christ! In Jesus, we
can know that all will be okay for He is greater than every
obstacle that we face!

A refuge from the storm
You are my place of shelter
When life goes awry
You are my center

Arrows fly by night
Attacks come by day
You're my place of shelter
My trafficless freeway!

Protected and safe
under the shadow of Your wings
From the sheltering place
hope and joy springs

Forth in my soul
I am renewed!
My heart fills with praise
so much gratitude

Come to the refuge
The invitation stands
He's got the whole world
safe in His hands!

Sitting at His Feet

> She had a sister called Mary, who
> sat at the Lord's feet listening to
> what he said. (Luke 10:39 NIV)

The place of the disciple is at the feet of Jesus! When we sit at the feet of Jesus, we acknowledge that He is our teacher and Lord. When we sit at the feet of Jesus, we can drink in all His love and His wisdom into our souls.

Sitting at His feet
listening to His Word
My soul is at rest
My heart is deeply stirred

With passion and peace
His sheep am I
All is well
when the Shepherd is nigh

Like Mary of Bethany
whose life of worship
Truly pleased the King
revealing His lordship

There's no place
that I'd rather be
than right here with You
Your love flowing freely

Your greatest command
is my heart's desire
To love You with passion
set me on fire!

Living at His Feet

> As Jesus and the disciples
> continued on their journey, they
> came to a village where a woman
> welcomed Jesus into her home.
> Her name was Martha and she
> had a sister named Mary. Mary
> sat down attentively before the
> Master, absorbing every revelation
> he shared. (Luke 10:38–39 TPT)

We are called to live at the feet of Jesus. This was Mary's posture. She sat at the feet of Jesus and took in all the Words that He spoke. It is the posture of the disciple. This is the place of worship and true intimacy with the Lord.

Living at Jesus's feet
I feel that I am home
Relishing the fact
that I am His own

A place where I can exhale
let all my worries go
A place where
I can be still and know

I simply ask
and the Spirit will dispense
Perfect peace fills me
Peace that makes no sense

Connected to the vine
I'm in another realm
Guided by His eye
He is at the helm

Come to His feet
Come, taste, and see
Experience life
as it was meant to be!

Eden

Eden was the place of paradise. It was paradise because it was the place of intimate communion and fellowship between God and His creation, Adam and Eve. Adam and Eve were driven from Eden because of their sin. Jesus came to restore our broken fellowship and intimacy with God. In doing so, Eden has been restored!

The Garden of Eden
where it all began
The perfect paradise
created for man (and woman!)

Walking with God
in the cool of the day
Intimate communion
filled with joy and play

Then there was the Fall
where they both took the fruit
Sin entered in
Now in need of a reboot

Jesus paid the price
so we could be restored
To give us back our lives
To live ashamed no more

Come back to Eden
Come home today
Come back to Communion
Jesus is the Way!

Jericho

> Now the gates of Jericho were tightly shut because the people were afraid of the Israelites. No one was allowed to go out or in. But the LORD said to Joshua, "I have given you Jericho, its king, and all its strong warriors." (Joshua 6:1–2 NLT)

Many of us learned about Joshua and the battle of Jericho when we were in Sunday school. It truly is an amazing, miraculous story of God's power on display. It teaches us that God's ways and strategies are often unorthodox and don't make sense from our human point of view. How can walls come tumbling down just by marching around them? What is the Jericho you are facing today? Embrace God's ways and strategies to secure the victory!

Joshua fought the battle
at Jericho
God's wisdom was displayed
His power He did show

God's ways
are higher than man's
So often different
from our earthly plans

Walk around the walls
then let out a shout
This is the key
to victory coming about

Joshua's role
was simply to obey
Doesn't make sense sometimes
This is God's way

Fight your Jericho
with the strategy God gives you
Obedience's the key ingredient
to experiencing a breakthrough!

Damascus

The road to Damascus was the place where the Risen Christ encountered and transformed the Apostle Paul. His name was changed from Saul to Paul. He went from being a persecutor of Christians to become the top proponent of the Christian faith. The same Lord encounters and transforms people today!

Damascus, the place
where Jesus encountered Paul
Totally changed
the man formerly known as Saul

The killer of Christians
became God's man
God can change anyone
by His powerful hand

The road to Damascus
The place where our pride
and our own agenda
fall by the wayside

The place of transformation
Where Jesus meets us where we are
Where we meet Him face-to-face
No longer from afar

Come to Damascus!
The Lord is waiting for you
Your life will not be the same
in Christ, you'll be made new!

Calvary

> "And when they had come to the place called Calvary, there they crucified Him, and the criminals, one on the right hand and the other on the left. (Luke 23:33 NKJV)

Calvary, the place where Jesus was crucified. Imagine yourself at Calvary today and stand in awe of our Savior dying on the cross for you. The hymn "Were you there when they crucified my Lord?" speaks of the awe and worship we experience at Calvary. Praise God for His awesome sacrifice for us on the cross of Calvary!

Everything was changed
on the mount called Calvary
Where Jesus died on the cross
Changed the course of history

The place where sins are forgiven
where He paid the price
For you and for me
The greatest sacrifice

Come to Calvary
and meet Jesus there
He extends His arms of love
showing you how much He cares

God demonstrates His love
by dying on the cross
He came to redeem
those who were lost

Calvary calls
to every person on earth
The ultimate price Jesus paid
shows our great worth.

Chapter 9

Dallas Willard Poems

Dallas Willard influenced my life in a very significant way. I took his two-week course in the doctor of ministry program at Fuller Seminary twice. It was an honor to know him personally as a spiritual mentor. More than any other mentor I've known, Dallas truly lived out the reality of the Kingdom and exuded the character of Jesus through the very pores of his being. One of his most helpful teachings for me was about releasing outcomes to the Lord. When we can truly release outcomes to the Lord, we can experience a worry-free, peaceful life in the Kingdom.

The Divine Conspiracy

He told them another parable.
"The kingdom of heaven is like
leaven that a woman took and hid
in three measures of flour, till it was
all leavened." (Matthew 13:33 ESV)

Dallas Willard taught us about the Divine Conspiracy that is taking place all around us. It is the conspiracy of God's Kingdom and His people that is working in our midst. The Kingdom of God is advancing forward and cannot be stopped! Though it cannot be seen, the Kingdom is at work in the lives of people all around the world. The King is drawing people to Himself. His Kingdom is eternal and everlasting!

The divine conspiracy
is in full swing!
Nothing can hinder
the rule of the King!

Jesus is Lord
in the King's domain
Surrender to Him
Come under His reign!

Jesus is the smartest
Man who ever lived!
Teaching us all
how to forgive

How to love our enemies
How to live in peace
How to live in freedom
in this life that does not cease

Join the conspiracy
Be part of His rule
Enroll today
in His discipleship school!

Renovation of My Heart

> Guard your heart above all else,
> for it determines the course of
> your life. (Proverbs 4:23 NLT)

God desires to transform our lives from the inside out. It all starts with the heart, for out of the heart flow the issues of life! Transform my heart of stone into a heart of flesh, Lord. Make my heart soft to the things on Your heart. With my heart, I choose to worship and follow You.

Lord, I need transformation
Renovation of my heart
Changing the way I think
This is where it starts

Transform my will, Lord
My soul's CEO
Help me to die to self
and let go of my ego

Spiritual disciplines
Help me to change
Training off the spot
My soul rearrange

Make my soul whole, Lord
Heal me from my wounds
With having my own way
may I not be consumed

Renovate my heart, Lord
This is my prayer
Releasing all outcomes
into Your good care!

Transforming Our Thoughts

And do not be conformed to this
world, but be transformed by
the renewing of your mind, that
you may prove what *is* that good
and acceptable and perfect will
of God. (Romans 12:2 NKJV)

Transform my thinking, Lord! I am daily bombarded with
the messages of the world. Messages that base my worth
on materialistic values. Messages that devalue me as a
person saying that I need to measure up to the world's
standards. Help my thinking to come into alignment with
the truth found in Your Word!

Transform my mind, Lord
Change the way I think
May I be in tune
with Your thoughts be in sync

May ideas and images
Be inspired by Your love
To fix my mind on You
To dwell on things above

Help me engage
in holy thinking
When I'm feeling down
When my soul starts sinking

Meditating upon
Your Holy living Word
May my faith increase
by what my soul has heard

May I think like Jesus
Absorb His brilliant mind
A mind that is transformed
A mind that is aligned!

Transforming Our Feelings

> So abandon every form
> of evil, deceit, hypocrisy,
> feelings of jealousy and
> slander. (1 Peter 2:1 TPT)

God has given us our feelings so we can experience life in its fullness. But living life on the basis of our feelings is not a good way to live. We need to walk by our faith and trust in God.

Lord, help me to walk by faith and not by my feelings. My feelings go up and down based upon the ever changing circumstances. Faith stands on the Word. May my feelings follow my faith in You!

Help me, O Lord
to master my feelings
So many times
they've become my ceiling

A blessing and a problem
feelings have so much power
One minute, I'm happy
The next, I am sour

Help me to keep
My feelings in their place
To not guide my life
yet give them their space

Lord, let the feelings
of Your joy and Your peace
Fill up my life
May they ever increase

Faith, hope, and love
On these I will stand
Lord, strengthen me
by Your right hand.

Transforming Our Will

> But if serving the LORD seems
> undesirable to you, then choose
> for yourselves this day whom
> you will serve, whether the gods
> your ancestors served beyond
> the Euphrates, or the gods of
> the Amorites, in whose land you
> are living. But as for me and
> my household, we will serve
> the LORD. (Joshua 24:15 NIV)

God gives us the freedom to choose- to choose to follow the Lord and His ways or to choose our own path. He woos us to relationship with Him and to follow His good plan for us.

I choose to follow You, Lord! Thank You for giving me a free will to choose to respond to Your great love for me. Help me to choose to think thoughts that are pleasing to you. Help me to obey Your Word by the power of Your Holy Spirit.

Transform my will, Lord
My self's CEO
Surrendered to You
Help me to flow

with You and Your Kingdom
May Your will be done
Letting go of my way
where the battle's won

Transform my splintered will
with its many desires
To will one thing
To You I aspire

From abandonment to contentment
to full participation
Wholly engaged with You
Let that be my station

The Lord is my Shepherd
I really do lack nothing
Teach me, Lord, how to live
the life of fully trusting!

Transforming Our Body

> Therefore, I urge you, brothers and
> sisters, in view of God's mercy,
> to offer your bodies as a living
> sacrifice, holy and pleasing to
> God—this is your true and proper
> worship. (Romans 12:1 NIV)

God has given each of us a body to live out God's purpose for our lives. Our bodies are described as Living Temples of the Holy Spirit; the very place where the Spirit of God dwells.

Lord, I present my body to You as a living sacrifice! I dedicate my body and its parts to be instruments of righteousness for Your Kingdom. May I use my body to serve You and to be a blessing to others.

I present my body, Lord
as a living sacrifice
For I'm not my own
I've been bought with a price

Transform my body, Lord
My personal power pack
Used for Your glory
May I stay on track

Through spiritual disciplines
help me to reign
Silence and solitude
Tools for me to train

To love my body
Kept in its place
For my body is me
a vessel of Your grace

Rule over my body, Lord
So I may be blessed
For Your yoke is easy
in You, I find rest!

Transforming Our Relationships

> A new command I give you:
> Love one another. As I have
> loved you, so you must love
> one another. (John 13:34 NIV)

God has called us all to live in community with one another. We are all part of God's eternal and holy family. Life is so much richer and fuller when we live in healthy relationships with others.

Lord, help us to love one another, the way that You have loved us! The only way we can do this is to receive afresh Your love for us. And then to let that love flow to ourselves and to others. Thank You, Lord, that Your supply of love is endless and everlasting!

Transform my relationships
May they be marked by love
The love called "agape"
from our Father above

Help me to end
attack and withdraw
To accept one another
when we show our flaws

Our God is love
That is who He is
When we love each other
we show that we are His

Help us, Lord, to love
We draw from Your well
We find our strength in You
in Your presence, we will dwell

By this, all will know
that we are His disciples
Loving one another
We are the living Bible!

Transforming Our Soul

> He restores my soul. He leads me in paths of righteousness for his name's sake. (Psalm 23:3 ESV)

Bless the Lord, O my soul! Let all that is within me bless Your holy Name! Bring restoration and healing to my soul, O Lord. May the parts of my soul that have been broken by people be renewed and restored by the power of Your Name!

Transform my soul, Lord
I place it under You
Knowing that You value
my "who" more than my "do"

Heal my broken pieces
Restore my soul today
Let Your love transform me
My fears You will allay

The character of Jesus
My soul it does aspire
Make me more like You
Set my heart on fire

My soul, my inner stream
that flows from within
Gushing living water
overflows the brim

My soul is satisfied
when I am in Your care
I commit my soul to You
This is my daily prayer!

Releasing Outcomes

And he said to all, "If anyone would come after me, let him deny himself and take up his cross daily and follow me." (Luke 9:23 ESV)

The Lord calls us to release all outcomes to Him. We must die to ourselves and our need for control. We need to trust in His goodness and mercy and leave the results in His hands.

Lord, we release outcomes to You. In doing so, there is such freedom and peace. We rest in Your goodness and trust that Your Will is best for our lives!

Releasing outcomes
Lord, set me free
Giving my burdens
over to Thee

Thy Kingdom come
Thy will be done
In my surrender
the battle is won

Your yoke is easy
Your burden is light
Living by faith
not with my sight

Whatever may come
You're in control
I trust in Your goodness
I don't trust the polls

I release all outcomes
Daily I repeat
Trusting in all things
In You, I'm complete!

Effort Not Earning

> For by grace you have been saved
> through faith. And this is not your
> own doing; it is the gift of God, not
> a result of works, so that no one
> may boast. (Ephesians 2:8–9 ESV)

Salvation is free; working out our salvation takes great effort! Yes, we are saved by grace through faith. But the grace that saves us will lead us to do good works. The grace that we receive brings transformation in our lives and causes us to do the good works that God has called us to do. These works require effort on our part; these works never earn our favor with God. They enable us to experience God's Kingdom in a tangible way.

Grace not opposed to effort
It's opposed to earning
We need to do our part
We must be discerning

Burning grace like gas
Fuel for my soul
Not just forgiveness
Power to make us whole

Dallas taught us all
How to train to reign
Through the disciplines
we can rewire our brain!

Life in the Kingdom
Eternal life is here
It's already begun
The call to follow clear

This is the good life
found in the Bible
It's the same now as then
The life of the disciple!

Chapter 10

Beatitudes Poems

The beatitudes give us such a clear picture of the qualities of the Kingdom citizen. They show us how we can access the abundant and unlimited resources of the Kingdom of God. These poems on the beatitudes will help us access these resources available to us!

Blessed Are the Poor in Spirit

> Blessed are the poor in spirit,
> for theirs is the kingdom of
> heaven. (Matthew 5:3 NIV)

The ways of the Kingdom are completely opposite from the ways of the world. The world values power, prestige, and prominence. God's Kingdom values humility, weakness, and poverty of spirit. These are the places where we can connect with God in a deep and powerful way. When we are poor in spirit we recognize our deep need for God. And how He responds to our need! When we come to Him in our poverty, we find treasure and riches in the Kingdom found nowhere else!

Blessed are the poor in spirit
For theirs is the Kingdom
For when we know our need
Then we find true freedom

Accessing the resources
The King has freely given
Live the life
that we're meant to be livin'

The values of the world
will drive you into the ground
The values of the Kingdom
will turn your life around

To die is to gain
To me, to live is Christ
Come and discover
the Pearl of Great Price

All who are poor in spirit
You're invited to His table
For the Lord is kind
He's loving, and He's faithful!

Blessed Are Those Who Mourn

> Blessed *are* those who mourn,
> For they shall be comforted.
> (Matthew 5:4 NKJV)

Those who mourn and are filled with sadness find heavenly comfort. This life is filled with so many painful things. Pain and suffering are part of this life on earth. The Good News is that when we come to God in our broken and hurting state we experience God's comfort and healing.

Lord, we come to you today with all our hurts and pains. Bring Your comfort to us afresh and heal us. Thank You that we can meet You in this raw place of our lives and find love and acceptance.

Blessed are those who mourn
Comfort they will find
In the love of Christ
their wounds He will bind

Weeping lasts the night
Joy comes in the morning
In our times of pain
Christ's image is forming

God is near those
who have broken hearts
He puts us back together
when we fall apart

He weeps with those who weep
He wipes away our tears
"It will be okay"
He whispers in our ears

There is a blessing
when we go through trials
Our nearness to the Lord
makes it all worthwhile!

Blessed Are the Meek

> Blessed are the meek, for they will inherit the earth. (Matthew 5:5 NIV)

Meekness is not weakness! Meekness is strength harnessed under God's control. Jesus possessed incredible fortitude yet was fully yielded to the Father. The times we are living in call for this quality of meekness. There is so much division and conflict in this world. When we relate to one another with a Spirit of meekness, relationships become so much more peaceful and harmonious! Lord, may we become more meek like You today!

Blessed are the meek
The earth they will inherit
A gift of God's grace
not their own merit

Strength under control
Meekness is defined
A heart that is yielded
A life that is aligned

Meekness is true strength
Meekness is not weak
of the spiritual kind
Not about physique

When under attack
the meek are even-keeled
The Lord is their defender
The Lord is their shield

Blessed are the meek
It is the better way
Walking humbly daily
On this path I'll stay!

Blessed Are Those Who Hunger and Thirst

Blessed are those who hunger and
thirst for righteousness, for they
will be filled. (Matthew 5:6 NIV)

When we hunger after the things of the world, we are left unfulfilled. When we hunger after God and His Kingdom, our souls are satisfied. The key is hungering for the right things! He has promised to fill up our souls with His Spirit and His blessings when we seek Him.

Lord, we hunger for You today. Increase our spiritual appetite for You and Your Kingdom. Fill us afresh with Your Spirit and with Your goodness in our lives.

Blessed are those who hunger
And thirst for righteousness
for they will be filled
They have Kingdom access

The God-shaped vacuum
in every human soul
can be filled only by God
Only He can make us whole

Hungering for God
more than worldly things
Satisfies the soul
Joy the Lord does bring

You cup will overflow
with many Kingdom blessings
Life will be peaceful
You won't be stressing

So grow your appetite
for God and His Word
You will taste and see
what no eye has seen nor ear has heard!

Blessed Are the Merciful

> Blessed *are* the merciful,
> For they shall obtain mercy.
> (Matthew 5:7 NKJV)

Thank God for His mercy in our lives! His mercies are new every morning. As we receive the mercy of God in our lives, we become conduits of His mercy to others. There is so much judgment and condemnation all around us. As givers and receivers of mercy, let us change the atmosphere in our world! It starts with one person at a time. May a new mercy wave swell and grow and touch all the peoples of the earth!

Blessed are the merciful
Mercy they will find
It's the cycle of blessing
It is God designed

The mercy of God
Freely poured out
Freely we receive
when we believe and do not doubt

Then mercy starts to flow
from us to others
Obeying God's command
To love one another

This is what the world needs
This cycle of grace
Breaking down the walls
that we have put in place

Lord, have mercy!
Pour it out afresh
Pour out Your Spirit
Upon all flesh!

Blessed Are the Pure in Heart

> Blessed are the pure in
> heart, for they will see God.
> (Matthew 5:8 NIV)

God has cleansed us by the precious blood of Jesus. We are made new and now have access to the very Presence of God. We can see Him clearly face to face. We can see Him clearly working in us and around us. This blessing of seeing God is available to every believer!

Blessed are the pure in heart
God they will see!
Their eyes are opened
to spiritual reality

For God is working
all the time
He's preparing wineskins
for the new wine

Cleansed by His blood
We boldly approach His throne
We find unconditional love
The place where we are known

With all diligence
Your heart you must guard
For from it flows everything
Don't let it grow hard

The pure in heart
Are truly blessed
For they will see
life at its best!

Blessed Are the Peacemakers

> Blessed are the peacemakers,
> for they will be called children
> of God. (Matthew 5:9 NIV)

The Prince of Peace, our Lord Jesus, has commissioned every believer to be a peacemaker! We have His Peace, His shalom, residing in our hearts. We are called to bring His shalom to every relationship, every circumstance in our lives. Lord, may Your peace overflow from our lives to this broken, hurting world.

Blessed are the peacemakers
for they are God's kids
They are the ones
who do what God bids

Ministers of reconciliation
who bring peace to others
Uniting humanity
We're sisters and brothers!

Through His blood on the cross
Jesus the peacemaker
broke down the walls
Became the sin breaker

We are all called
to be makers of peace
In this world that's at war
the violence needs to cease!

The world needs God's peace
now more than ever!
Blessed are the peacemakers
God bless their endeavors!

Blessed Are the Persecuted

> Blessed are those who are
> persecuted because of
> righteousness, for theirs is
> the kingdom of heaven.
> (Matthew 5:10 NIV)

Following Jesus includes suffering for the Kingdom. It is a part of every disciple's life. They persecuted our Lord Jesus and His disciples when He walked this earth. He told us to expect persecution when we follow Him. The Good News is that when we are persecuted we find that our walk with the Lord deepens. Not only that, our Lord said that we would be rewarded in heaven when we do suffer for His Name's sake. What a good and faithful Lord we serve!

Blessed are the persecuted
Who suffer for the Kingdom
Who take a courageous stand
Whatever may come

they shall be rewarded
Their suffering not in vain
All of their losses
will one day be gain

Jesus said His followers
would suffer loss
Just like He did
He went to the cross!

As we follow Jesus
be prepared to suffer
and as we do
may His peace be our buffer

In this world
we will have tribulation
Jesus has overcome
Join the celebration!